Manuscryptha©Copyright 2025

All rights reserved.

Protected with www.protectmywork.com,

The material within this book may not be copied, reproduced, or shared in any form without explicit written permission from the author or publisher.

Under no circumstances shall the author or publisher be held liable for any damages, financial losses, or other consequences resulting directly or indirectly from the information provided in this book.

Legal Notice:

This book is protected by copyright and is intended for personal use only. You may not modify, distribute, sell, quote, or reproduce any portion of its content without prior consent from the author or publisher.

Disclaimer:

The content in this book is meant solely for educational and entertainment purposes. Every effort has been made to ensure that the information is accurate, current, and reliable. However, no guarantees or warranties, either expressed or implied, are provided.

Readers acknowledge that the author is not offering legal, financial, medical, or professional advice. The content is derived from various sources, and it is strongly recommended to consult a licensed professional before attempting any methods outlined in this book.

By reading this material, you agree that the author is not responsible for any direct or indirect losses resulting from the use of the information contained within, including errors, omissions, or inaccuracies.

The Gospel of Mary Magdalene

A Complete Guide to the Her Lost Text, Forbidden Wisdom, and the Return of the Divine Feminine

Presented, Introduced, and Contextualized by Rush Nilson

Author Mary Magdalene

TABLE OF CONTENTS

1 - INTRODUCTION 1

2 - A FORGOTTEN GOSPEL AND A HIDDEN TRUTH 5
2.1 Why was The Gospel of Mary lost for centuries? 6
2.2 What makes it unique compared to other apocryphal gospels? 8

3 - THE REDISCOVERY OF THE GOSPEL OF MARY 11
3.1 Where was the text found, and why was it hidden for so long? 12
3.2 The Codex Berolinensis 8502 – the main manuscript 14
3.3 The Greek fragments from Oxyrhynchus and Manchester 17
3.4 The missing sections and textual reconstruction challenges 19

4 - THE CONTENT OF THE GOSPEL OF MARY 21
4.2 Mary Magdalene as Jesus' closest disciple 23
4.3 The soul's journey and its vision of the cosmos 26
4.4 More Than One Meaning: Magdalene as Apostle and Archetype 28
4.5 The conflict with Peter and the debate over her authority 32

5 – THE THEOLOGICAL AND PHILOSOPHICAL THEMES   35

    5.2 The concept of inner knowledge (gnosis) as the path to salvation   37

    5.3 A different understanding of sin and redemption compared to canonical Gospels   39

    5.4 Spiritual freedom as the core message of the text   41

    5.5 Other Gospels, Other Voices   42

       The Gospel of Thomas   44

       The Gospel of Philip   46

       The Gospel of Judas   48

       Pistis Sophia   50

       The Gospel of Truth   52

6 – MAGDALENE AND SOPHIA: ECHOES OF THE DIVINE FEMININE
    54

    6.1 Wisdom in Exile: Sophia in the Biblical and Gnostic Traditions   55

    6.2 A Mirror in Magdalene: Parallels Between Two Silenced Voices   57

    6.3 The Return of the Sacred Feminine   59

    6.4 Knowledge as Reunion, Not Control   61

7 – WHY WAS THE GOSPEL OF MARY EXCLUDED?   63

    7.1 Why was this gospel not included in the New Testament?   64

    7.2 The role of oral tradition and manuscript transmission   66

    7.3 The issue of female authority in early Christianity   67

    7.4 Early critiques of Mary Magdalene in patristic writings   69

8 – HOW TO READ THIS TEXT   71

    8.1 A living text, not a dead document   72

8.2 Reading with openness and without dogma	73
8.3 What to notice while reading	74
8.4 A text for Seekers	75

9 – THE GOSPEL OF MARY MAGDALENE — 77

Introduction to the Text	78
Pages 1-6	78
Page 7 - CH. 4	78
Pages 11-14	81
Pages 15 - CH. 8	83

10 – CONCLUSION: THE ENDURING LEGACY OF THE GOSPEL OF MARY — 87

10.1 A Voice That Refuses to Be Silenced	88
10.2 Beyond History: What This Gospel Leaves Us With	89
10.3 The Open Question: What Comes Next?	91
10.4 The Path of Magdalene	92
Stories That Travelled Far	92
Sacred Places and Silent Devotion	95
When Legend Carries Truth	97

APPENDIX:
ECHOES OF THE FEMININE LIGHT — 99

Thunder, Perfect Mind	102
Introduction to Thunder, Perfect Mind	102
Part I - The Divine Mirror	103
Part II - The Hidden Dance of Presence and Absence	106
The Gospel of Philip	110
Introduction to The Gospel of Philip	110
Part I - Awakening to the Light from Illusion to Remembrance	110
Part II - The Journey from Division to Divine Union	114
Part III - Light, Silence, and the True Way	116
Part IV - The Living Flame: Encountering the Divine Beyond Ritual	117
Final Note	118

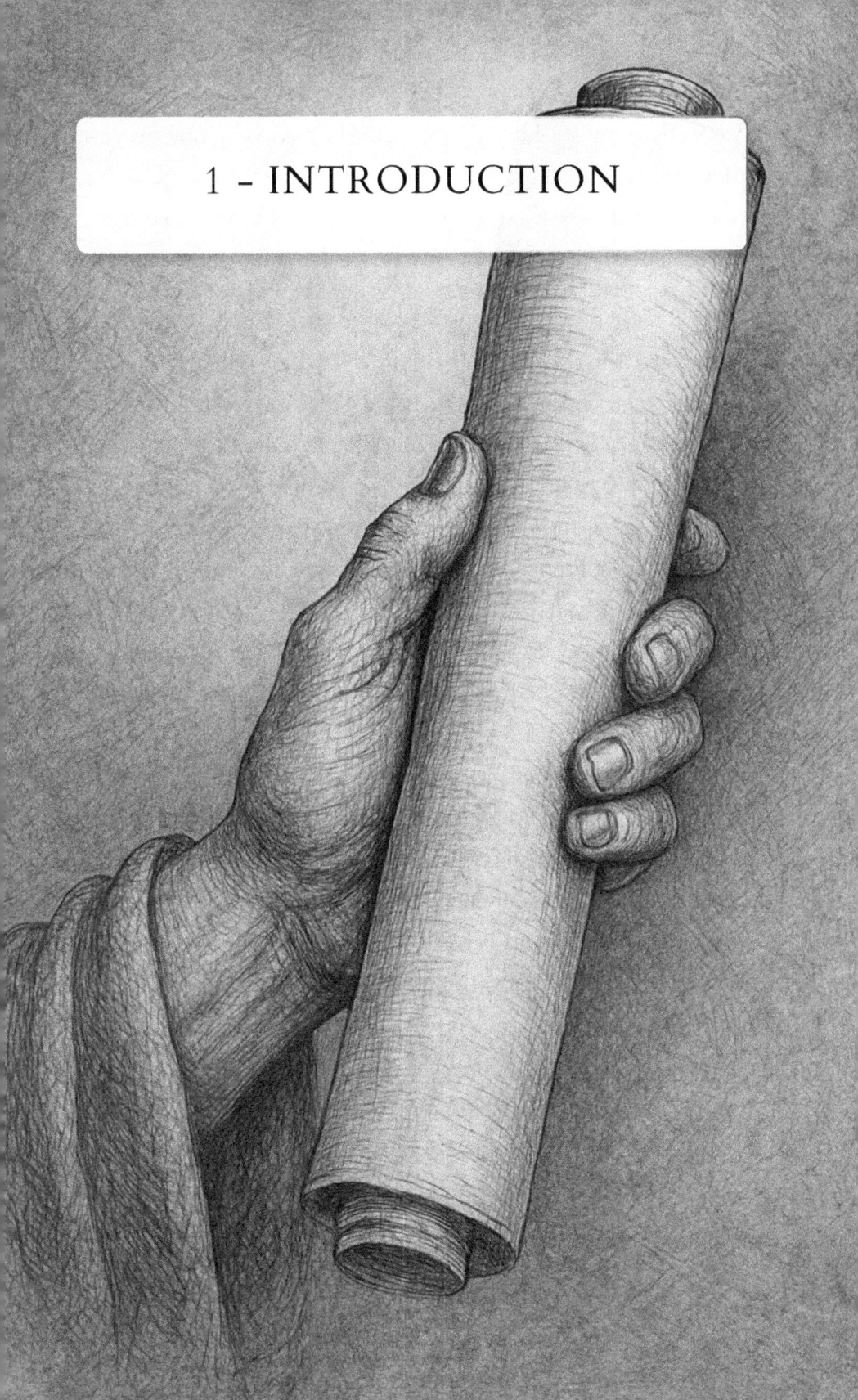

1 - INTRODUCTION

Some texts never fully disappear. They survive not because they were meant to—but because someone, somewhere, remembered. The Gospel of Mary is one of those rare voices, once silenced, that found a way to speak again.

Discovered in the sands of Egypt in a time when few cared to listen, the Gospel of Mary is both a mystery and a mirror. It's a mystery because we still don't know who wrote it, when exactly it was composed, or what its complete form may have looked like. Only fragments remain—parts missing, voices broken mid-sentence. And yet, it remains a mirror: reflecting a vision of early Christianity that challenges what many of us thought we knew. It offers a portrait of Mary Magdalene not as a mere companion to Jesus, but as a trusted teacher, a revealer of hidden wisdom, and perhaps even a spiritual equal. That alone is enough to stir the imagination. But there's more. This gospel doesn't just reclaim Mary's voice—it reimagines what spiritual authority could look like. Unlike the canonical gospels, which often focus on external acts, commandments, and hierarchies, the Gospel of Mary is inward-looking. Its central theme is a journey of the soul. Salvation here is not granted by obedience or sacrifice, but by knowledge—personal, interior, experiential. It is a text concerned with what it means to truly see, to know, to awaken. We must be honest: this gospel is not easy. Not because it's full of obscure doctrine or complex theology, but because it asks something radical of us. It asks us to reconsider what has been left out. It invites us to wonder why certain texts were preserved, copied, and canonized—while others, like this one, were buried, forgotten, or declared heretical. The Gospel of Mary doesn't shout. It doesn't condemn. It simply speaks, quietly and with deep conviction, from across the centuries. And in doing so, it raises difficult and beautiful questions. What would Christianity look like if this gospel had not been lost? What if Mary's voice had been allowed to echo alongside Matthew, Mark, Luke, and John? How would our understanding of sin, salvation, and the soul have changed? To ask these questions is not to reject tradition, but to enrich it. The Gospel of Mary doesn't contradict the canonical texts—it complements them in surprising ways. It doesn't seek to tear down faith, but to deepen it. And for many who encounter this text for the first time, the experience is not one of rebellion, but of recognition. It's as if something long silent has stirred, something that speaks not just to the mind, but to the heart.Reading the Gospel of Mary today means entering into a conversation that is both ancient and current. In a time when questions about authority, gender, and spiritual authenticity are more urgent than ever, this text offers a voice that is refreshingly bold, yet profoundly humble. It is a gospel of paradox: silent for centuries, yet still speaking; forgotten by history, yet remembered by intuition. What follows in the pages ahead is not just the story of a lost gospel. It is the story of how it was found again. It is the story of its strange journey from a crumbling papyrus in a forgotten library to the shelves of scholars, theologians, and seekers. It is also a careful reading of what remains of the text—line by line, with context and commentary—and a meditation on what its message might mean for us today. Before we enter the gospel itself, we will look first at the questions surrounding it. Where did it come from? Why was it lost? What makes it so different from other early Christian writings? And perhaps most importantly: what was so dangerous about Mary Magdalene's voice that it had to be silenced? This book is not written for specialists only. It is for anyone who has ever wondered whether the Christian story is broader than we were told. It is for those who sense that something essential may have been left out—not through malice, but through time, politics, and the very human act of forgetting. It is for those drawn to the quiet wisdom of the hidden, the marginal, the nearly erased. You don't need to believe anything to read the Gospel of Mary. You only need curiosity. This gospel doesn't demand faith in doctrines. It invites trust in your own capacity to perceive, to question, to seek. In that sense, it is not a relic of the past, but a companion for the present. It walks beside those who refuse to give up on wonder. So let us begin—not just with analysis, but with openness. With reverence for what has endured, and curiosity for what it still has to teach. The Gospel of Mary waited a long time to be heard again. Now that it has returned, the question is no longer whether we will find it—but whether we are ready to listen.

2 – A FORGOTTEN GOSPEL AND A HIDDEN TRUTH

2.1 WHY WAS THE GOSPEL OF MARY LOST FOR CENTURIES?

The disappearance of the Gospel of Mary was not the result of a single dramatic event—no public condemnation, no official decree of destruction. It vanished in the quiet way many things do: through neglect, disinterest, and the shifting winds of power. For nearly fifteen hundred years, no one read its words aloud, no scribes copied its lines, no voices carried its message forward. The text slipped away not in flames, but in silence.

To understand why, we must look to the early centuries of Christianity—a period far more diverse and complex than many assume. In the first few generations after Jesus' death, there was no unified theology, no fixed canon, no centralized church. There were only communities—scattered, passionate, creative—each trying to make sense of what they believed had happened, and what it meant.

Some communities focused on law and continuity with Jewish tradition. Others leaned into mystical visions, apocalyptic hope, or personal revelation. The Gospel of Mary likely emerged in one of the latter groups—communities that emphasized inner knowledge (gnosis), spiritual equality, and the idea that salvation came not from hierarchy or ritual, but from awakening.

But as Christianity moved from a persecuted minority to a growing institutional force, the need for cohesion grew stronger. Diversity, once tolerated, became problematic. Writings that didn't align with emerging orthodox positions—especially those that gave central authority to figures like Mary Magdalene—began to fall out of favor. Over time, these texts were not copied. Libraries were reorganized. Memory narrowed.

And yet, it wasn't only theology that worked against Mary's gospel. It was politics. Mary Magdalene, in this text, speaks as a teacher, a visionary, and a disciple with access to hidden knowledge. She is depicted as someone Jesus trusted deeply—perhaps more than the others. This directly challenged the authority of Peter and the male-dominated leadership that came to define the early church. In the Gospel of Mary, Peter himself is portrayed as skeptical of Mary's role, asking, "Did he really speak with a woman in private?" Her authority is not assumed—it is questioned.

Texts that placed women in positions of leadership were rarely welcomed by the institutional church. They threatened not only doctrine, but structure. The Gospel of Mary, in suggesting a model of spiritual insight unbound by gender or clerical mediation, quietly undermined the logic of the growing ecclesiastical system.

And so it faded—not by force, but by omission.

What's remarkable is that it survived at all. That a copy of it was buried in Egypt and rediscovered in the late 19th century is, in itself, an act of quiet defiance against time. The partial manuscript we now have—written in Coptic, translated from Greek, possibly based on an even earlier tradition—reminds us that history is not only written by the victors. Sometimes, it's rewritten by those who refuse to let certain voices disappear.

The Gospel of Mary wasn't lost because it was irrelevant. It was lost because it was too relevant—too challenging, too unorthodox, too bold in what it implied about knowledge, power, and the role of women. That makes its return not just an archaeological event, but a spiritual one.

2.2 WHAT MAKES IT UNIQUE COMPARED TO OTHER APOCRYPHAL GOSPELS?

Among the many so-called apocryphal gospels—texts written outside the New Testament but attributed to early Christian figures—the Gospel of Mary stands apart. While others often expand on Jesus' miracles, offer childhood stories, or provide secret teachings, this gospel is radically different in tone, structure, and intention. It doesn't try to tell a story about Jesus. Instead, it tells us something about the soul—and about Mary herself.

The first striking element is its voice. Unlike most early Christian writings, where women are marginal or silent, here Mary speaks. She doesn't merely echo Jesus' teachings—she interprets them. She comforts the other disciples, offers insight, and shares a vision revealed to her alone. She is not portrayed as a helper or passive witness, but as a leader in her own right. In this, the gospel re-centers the narrative around a woman who, in most other texts, is sidelined.

Equally significant is what the Gospel of Mary doesn't do. There is no crucifixion scene, no resurrection narrative, no miracles, no mention of Jesus as the Messiah in the traditional sense. Instead, it focuses on a conversation between Jesus and his disciples after his resurrection—followed by a vision Mary shares with the group. The emphasis is not on historical events but on spiritual understanding. Salvation, in this gospel, is not tied to blood sacrifice or divine intervention, but to inner transformation.

This is where the gospel aligns with what scholars often call "gnostic tendencies"—though it's important to note that the Gospel of Mary is not a full-fledged Gnostic text. It does not describe a complex cosmology or multiple divine beings. But it shares the gnostic emphasis on personal revelation, the idea that truth is found through knowing, not through doctrine. In this view, the soul journeys upward through layers of ignorance and desire, ultimately returning to its origin. Mary's vision in the text illustrates this process beautifully and symbolically.

Another unique feature is the tone of conflict within the community. Most gospels present the disciples as a unified group. Here, however, there is tension. Peter questions Mary's authority, implying that Jesus would never entrust his teachings to a woman. Levi defends her, challenging Peter's assumptions and pointing to the value of inner worth over external status. This candid portrayal of early disagreement suggests that the author was not writing to smooth things over, but to capture something real—perhaps a debate still alive in their own community.

Lastly, the Gospel of Mary is not interested in building a church or establishing rituals. It doesn't command obedience or demand allegiance to any institution. Instead, it speaks to the individual soul, urging inner peace, self-awareness, and freedom from illusion. The true "Son of Humanity," Jesus says, is found not in the heavens but within you.

That message, quiet and daring, is what makes this gospel unique. It offers no miracles to believe in, no punishments to fear. Just a voice—Mary's voice—pointing inward, asking us not to follow her, but to awaken ourselves.

3 – THE REDISCOVERY OF THE GOSPEL OF MARY

CODEX BEROLINENSIS 8502

3.1 WHERE WAS THE TEXT FOUND, AND WHY WAS IT HIDDEN FOR SO LONG?

The Gospel of Mary came back to light not through a moment of grand revelation, but through dust, fragments, and the slow work of scholars. It was discovered in 1896 in Egypt, in a private collection of ancient texts bought on the antiquities market by a German diplomat named Carl Reinhardt. The manuscript was a papyrus codex—written in Coptic, the Egyptian language using Greek letters—later known as the Codex Berolinensis 8502.

At first, no one seemed to grasp what they had found. The manuscript sat relatively untouched in the Berlin Museum for decades, surviving even the bombing of Berlin in World War II. Only in the 1950s did scholars begin to study and translate it seriously. And when they did, they realized it was something extraordinary: a gospel unlike any other—attributed not to a male apostle, but to Mary.

The text was incomplete. The first six pages were missing, as were ten pages later in the manuscript. What we have begins mid-conversation and ends abruptly. But even so, the surviving content is rich and thought-provoking. It consists of two parts: a dialogue between Jesus and his disciples after the resurrection, and a vision Mary shares with them after he departs.

The manuscript was likely copied in the 5th century CE, but most scholars agree it is a translation of an earlier Greek original, probably written in the 2nd century. That makes it one of the earliest Christian writings outside the New Testament—and one of the few where a woman plays the central role.

Why was it hidden so long? Partly by accident. Egypt's dry climate preserved many early Christian texts, especially in monasteries and burial sites. But this text was not buried in the sand like the Nag Hammadi library; it was part of a private collection, passed through unknown hands, stored in obscurity. It wasn't destroyed—it was simply overlooked.

Yet there's also another answer. This gospel may have been intentionally set aside. The early Christian movement was not monolithic, and by the 4th century, the dominant church had begun to draw clear lines between what was "orthodox" and what was not. Writings that didn't support the developing canon or church hierarchy were excluded—and often forgotten. A gospel centered on inner knowledge, featuring a woman as the voice of authority, would have been an awkward fit.

So the Gospel of Mary survived in silence, copied perhaps for a community that treasured it even after it was pushed to the margins. Its preservation is a quiet miracle: not because it was hidden from danger, but because someone cared enough to copy it, preserve it, and pass it along.

When it was finally read again in the 20th century, it was as if a voice had returned from the edge of history—soft, clear, and utterly unexpected.

3.2 THE CODEX BEROLINENSIS 8502 – THE MAIN MANUSCRIPT

To understand how the Gospel of Mary has reached us, we must turn our attention to a single, fragile manuscript: the Codex Berolinensis 8502. This codex is more than just a physical object—it is a time capsule, a quiet vessel carrying voices across centuries. Without it, we wouldn't even know the Gospel of Mary existed.

Codex Berolinensis 8502 is a papyrus manuscript written in Coptic, the late Egyptian language used by Christians in Egypt, and dates to the 5th century CE. It is housed in the Egyptian Museum of Berlin, hence the name "Berolinensis." It contains four texts, all bound together in one volume:

1. The Apocryphon of John (a gnostic dialogue between Jesus and John),
2. The Gospel of Mary,
3. The Sophia of Jesus Christ,
4. The Act of Peter.

What these writings have in common is their concern with personal revelation, inner wisdom, and resistance to institutional authority. This gives us a clue about the community that may have cherished and preserved them. These weren't random texts thrown together—they were likely copied by a Christian group that valued non-canonical teachings and esoteric interpretations of Jesus' message.

The Gospel of Mary occupies the second position in the codex. Sadly, the beginning and middle portions are damaged or missing. The text starts mid-sentence and skips several pages in the middle—ten folios, to be precise. What remains covers about eight pages of Coptic text, which corresponds to a small but powerful message. Scholars estimate that, if complete, the gospel may have been 14–18 pages long—still brief, but packed with meaning.

The manuscript itself is not luxurious. It was written on inexpensive papyrus, probably by a non-professional scribe. The handwriting is relatively rough, with no illustrations or decorative elements. This tells us that the codex was not meant for show. It was created to be read and used—perhaps passed between readers in secret, perhaps kept safe in a private library or monastic setting where such texts could still be appreciated without fear of condemnation.

Its survival is remarkable. While other early Christian manuscripts were discovered in the sands of Nag Hammadi in jars or tombs, Codex Berolinensis was preserved above ground, likely moved from place to place before arriving in Cairo. It was acquired by Carl Reinhardt in 1896 during an expedition to Egypt and then brought to Germany. For decades, however, the codex was barely studied. Its importance wasn't fully recognized until the mid-20th century.

The fragility of this codex also reminds us how easily history could have gone another way. A single flood, a careless hand, a fire during wartime—and this gospel might have been lost forever. That it survived the chaos of centuries, including World War II bombings in Berlin, is nothing short of astonishing.

Thanks to this modest and worn manuscript, we have direct access to a text that redefines how we see Mary Magdalene—and perhaps, how we understand early Christianity itself. Codex Berolinensis 8502 is not just a historical artifact. It is, in a way, a quiet act of resistance. In preserving this gospel, it preserved a voice that challenges us even today.

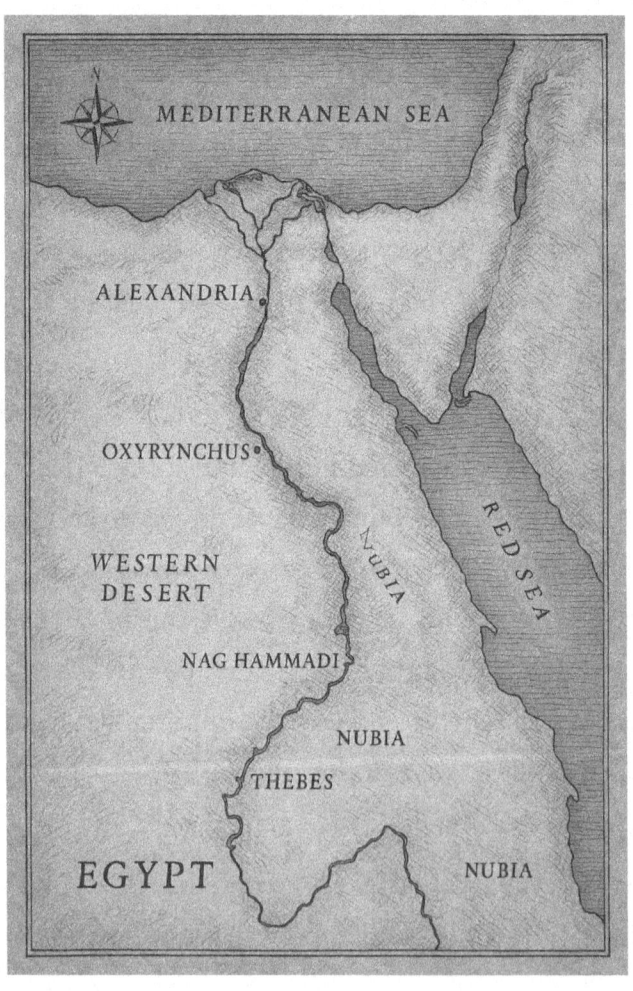

3.3 THE GREEK FRAGMENTS FROM OXYRHYNCHUS AND MANCHESTER

The Gospel of Mary is most widely known through the Coptic manuscript of Codex Berolinensis, but that's not the only witness we have. In the early 20th century, scholars discovered two Greek fragments of the same gospel—small, incomplete, but deeply significant. Found in different places, they confirm that this gospel had a broader circulation than once imagined, and that it likely existed first in Greek before being translated into Coptic.

The first fragment was unearthed in Oxyrhynchus, a city in Middle Egypt that became famous for its vast cache of papyri buried in ancient rubbish heaps. This fragment is part of the Oxyrhynchus Papyri Collection and is now housed at Oxford. It consists of a small portion of the Gospel of Mary, written in Greek, and is dated to the early 3rd century, possibly even late 2nd century. Though only a few lines long, the content aligns with the middle portion of the Coptic version, confirming that this gospel was already in circulation well before the 5th-century manuscript we depend on today.

The second Greek fragment was found in a much less expected place: Manchester, England. It was discovered in the John Rylands Library, among a collection of miscellaneous papyri. Like the Oxyrhynchus piece, it's short and damaged, but the text overlaps with the known Coptic version, reinforcing the gospel's existence in multiple communities. This fragment is also dated to the 3rd century, placing it within a generation or two of the earliest Christian writings outside the New Testament canon.

What do these fragments tell us? First, they show that the Gospel of Mary had an earlier and more diverse history than some assumed. The Greek language was the common medium of intellectual and religious writing in the eastern Roman Empire, especially in urban Christian centers like Alexandria. That the gospel existed in Greek suggests that its audience may have included educated, Hellenized Christians—people open to philosophical interpretations of faith and interested in teachings that moved beyond surface-level doctrine.

Second, these fragments support the idea that the Coptic version is not the original, but a translation from a Greek source. Some of the language and phrasing in the Coptic manuscript, when back-translated into Greek, flows more naturally—evidence that the gospel, like many early Christian texts, began its journey in the lingua franca of the time.

Finally, the very existence of multiple fragments from different locations suggests that the Gospel of Mary was copied and read in more than one community. It may not have been mainstream, but it was not entirely fringe either. It traveled. It was read. It mattered.

Like echoes from a broken vase, these small pieces don't tell us everything—but they tell us enough to know that this gospel once had a life beyond the margins, a place in the conversation that early Christianity was having with itself.

3.4 THE MISSING SECTIONS AND TEXTUAL RECONSTRUCTION CHALLENGES

Reading the Gospel of Mary is like stepping into a conversation already in progress—and then suddenly, midway, losing the signal. The manuscript we possess is deeply fragmented, with two major lacunae: the first six pages are entirely missing, and ten pages are gone from the middle of the text, right after Mary begins recounting her revelatory vision.

This poses a unique challenge to anyone seeking to understand the gospel in its entirety. The first missing section likely contained the beginning of the dialogue between Jesus and his disciples following his resurrection. We catch only the tail end of this exchange in the surviving text, where Jesus urges them not to be led by external laws, but to seek inner peace. What preceded that? Did he speak more extensively about the soul? About Mary herself? About what would happen next? We don't know—but the questions linger.

The second and larger gap is particularly frustrating for scholars and readers alike. It comes just as Mary begins to describe a vision shown to her by the Savior. She speaks of the soul's ascent past cosmic powers—figures called Desire, Ignorance, and Wrath. But then, abruptly, ten pages are missing. The manuscript resumes mid-thought, and we are left with only fragments of her journey. We can guess that the missing text likely described additional confrontations or teachings, but any such guess remains speculative.

These gaps are not just a loss of information; they also change how we engage with the gospel. They create a sense of mystery, but also demand humility. We are not reading a finished, polished account. We are working with what has survived—what chance and time have allowed us to hold.

Over the years, many scholars have tried to reconstruct the missing parts, either by drawing from thematic parallels in other Gnostic or apocryphal texts, or by attempting to restore likely Greek phrases behind the Coptic translation. Some suggest that the missing opening might have resembled the beginnings of other post-resurrection dialogues, such as those found in the Gospel of Thomas or the Dialogue of the Savior. Others have speculated that the missing vision sequences might have drawn more explicitly on Platonic or mystical cosmologies.

But such reconstructions remain hypothetical. The truth is: we don't know what was there. And maybe that's part of the gospel's strange power. Its gaps force us to slow down, to reflect, to read between the lines. They invite us to fill the silence not with doctrine, but with our own questions.

In a way, the Gospel of Mary speaks not only through what it says, but through what it has lost. Its brokenness mirrors the spiritual journey it describes—a path not of certainty, but of seeking, fragment by fragment, toward wholeness.

4 – THE CONTENT OF THE GOSPEL OF MARY

4.1 WHAT DOES THIS GOSPEL ACTUALLY SAY?

Stripped of later dogmas, rituals, and theological systems, the Gospel of Mary offers something simple, even startling: a conversation. It begins in the quiet aftermath of the resurrection. Jesus has just spoken to his disciples—not in parables, not in commands, but in words that center on inner peace, self-knowledge, and freedom from fear.

The gospel opens mid-discourse. Jesus is responding to a question about sin and how to overcome it. His answer is striking: sin, he says, is not a punishment from God or the result of broken laws. Rather, it arises from confusion—"from the mixing of natures." The world is not fallen, but fragmented, and healing comes not through sacrifice or law, but through understanding. "There is no sin," he says, "but it is you who make sin when you do the things that are like the nature of adultery." His words unsettle, because they redirect the entire problem of human failure inward.

He then tells his disciples to seek the inner self, to become fully human by knowing the truth within them. Then, as quickly as he appears, he departs—leaving the disciples afraid and confused. It is Mary who comforts them. She reminds them of the Savior's words, of the peace he offered, and she steps forward to share a vision he revealed to her in private.

In this vision—partially preserved—Mary describes the soul's ascent after death. It passes through spiritual powers that challenge it with questions and accusations. Each gatekeeper represents an obstacle: Desire, Ignorance, Wrath, and others unnamed. But the soul responds with clarity and detachment, shedding the burdens of each realm, until it reaches rest. It is a cosmic allegory for inner liberation.

What follows is tension. Peter challenges Mary's authority. "Did he really speak privately with a woman and not openly to us?" he asks, in disbelief. Mary weeps, but Levi defends her, affirming that she is worthy and that the Savior loved her more than the others. He urges the disciples to go and preach—not by authority, but by heart.

And then, the gospel ends.

No miracles. No Passion. No institutional blueprint. Just a call to awaken, and a woman's voice rising through fear and resistance, quietly insisting: what you seek is already within you.

4.2 MARY MAGDALENE AS JESUS' CLOSEST DISCIPLE

Among all the figures who orbit around Jesus in early Christian literature, Mary Magdalene remains one of the most compelling—and most contested. The canonical gospels describe her as a faithful follower, present at the crucifixion and the first to witness the resurrection. But the Gospel of Mary takes her far beyond that role. Here, she is not merely a witness. She is a disciple among disciples, a teacher, and perhaps even the one who understands Jesus best.

The text portrays Mary not just as close to Jesus, but as the one who receives a private revelation from him—something no other disciple claims in this gospel. After Jesus departs, the remaining disciples are left in fear and confusion. It is Mary who steps forward to reassure them, recalling the Savior's words and urging them not to lose heart. This is not the Mary of passive devotion. This is a Mary with clarity, authority, and memory. She is the one who remembers what the others seem to forget.

When the disciples ask her to share what Jesus told her in secret, she doesn't hesitate. She recounts a vision of the soul's ascent, in which spiritual obstacles are overcome through detachment, knowledge, and inner peace. This is not second-hand theology. Mary is not quoting scripture. She is interpreting, teaching, guiding—something we typically associate with Peter, Paul, or John in traditional Christian narratives. But here, the spiritual authority rests on Mary.

This prominence is not accidental. It reflects a different current in early Christianity—one in which women could be teachers, where discipleship was based on understanding rather than gender or status. In this current, Mary emerges not just as a "special" follower of Jesus, but as his closest confidante, the one he trusted with truths that others were not yet ready to hear.

The text makes this tension explicit. After Mary shares her vision, Peter challenges her. "Did he really speak with a woman in private, and not openly to us?" he asks, his tone dripping with suspicion. The challenge is not just about Mary's words—it's about her right to speak at all. His question reveals an underlying discomfort: how could a woman hold a place of such importance?

Mary is visibly shaken. She weeps. But before the moment collapses into silence or shame, another voice rises—Levi. He rebukes Peter, not with aggression but with reason. He reminds the group that if the Savior found her worthy, then they have no right to reject her. "Surely the Savior knows her very well," Levi says, "That is why he loved her more than us." With these words, the gospel affirms Mary's place—not as a tolerated exception, but as a chosen messenger.

This dynamic is powerful not just for what it says about Mary, but for what it reveals about the early church's internal tensions. The question of female leadership, of who could speak with authority, was not a later issue imposed by institutions. It was already present in the earliest circles of Jesus' followers. The Gospel of Mary offers a glimpse into those debates, unfiltered by centuries of theological smoothing.

And Mary, through all of this, does not seek dominance. She does not demand to be believed. She shares what she knows, speaks her truth, and accepts the resistance with sorrow but not defeat. Her strength lies not in power, but in quiet confidence—a sense that what she has seen and heard is true, regardless of who listens.

In reclaiming her voice, the Gospel of Mary also reclaims a vision of discipleship rooted not in status, but in wisdom, courage, and inner clarity. It presents a Jesus who entrusts his deepest teachings to the one most able to receive them—and a Mary who bears that responsibility with grace, even when the room doubts her. She is, in the truest sense, a disciple. And perhaps, in this gospel at least, the disciple.

4.3 THE SOUL'S JOURNEY AND ITS VISION OF THE COSMOS

At the heart of the Gospel of Mary lies one of its most profound and poetic moments: Mary's vision of the soul's ascent. It is here that the gospel shifts from conversation to revelation, offering a symbolic map of the spiritual journey—not of history or doctrine, but of the inner self's path toward liberation.

In her vision, Mary describes the soul's passage through four levels of resistance, each personified by a cosmic force: Desire, Ignorance, Wrath, and one unnamed. These are not demons in the traditional sense, but psychological or spiritual obstacles—conditions of the fallen human state that seek to pull the soul back into illusion and attachment.

Each figure challenges the soul with questions, accusations, or temptations. Desire demands, "Where are you going?" Ignorance tries to confuse, to bind the soul with falsehood. Wrath is aggressive, trying to dominate. But the soul responds with clarity and detachment, saying: "I saw you, but you did not see me." It refuses to be defined by fear or by false identity. It has remembered its origin.

This part of the gospel is deeply allegorical, and likely influenced by both Platonic philosophy and mystical Judaism. But it is also profoundly psychological. The soul's journey is not just about life after death—it is about the daily struggle to overcome ego, illusion, fear, and craving. It is about waking up.

What's striking is that the soul does not rely on angels, rituals, or external salvation. It liberates itself through knowledge, through insight. The ascent is an inner victory, achieved not by force but by understanding.

The missing pages of the manuscript interrupt the full sequence, leaving us to imagine what further insights Mary may have shared. But what we have is enough to feel the pulse of the message: freedom is possible, but it begins within.

In this vision, the gospel speaks not to institutions or beliefs, but to the traveler in each of us—the part that longs to return to something whole, something real. It is not a cosmic drama enacted in heaven, but an inner revolution, quietly unfolding in the soul of anyone who dares to see.

4.4 MORE THAN ONE MEANING: MAGDALENE AS APOSTLE AND ARCHETYPE

When we speak of Mary Magdalene, we are not only speaking of a historical figure—we are also engaging with a symbol, a presence, a possibility. Over the centuries, the layers of her identity have multiplied, revealing how deeply she continues to stir both scholarly inquiry and spiritual imagination. Among the many ways to understand her, two stand out: as an apostle, a woman who walked alongside Jesus and carried forward his message, and as an archetype, a representation of divine wisdom, inner transformation, and spiritual authority.

The first view—Mary as apostle—is grounded in history, or at least in the fragments that history has preserved. The canonical gospels present her as a follower of Jesus, a witness to his crucifixion, and the first to encounter him after the resurrection. In the Gospel of John, she is the one who is called by name, who recognizes him not with her eyes but with her heart. This intimate moment gives her a singular role in the resurrection story—so singular, in fact, that many in the early church referred to her as apostola apostolorum, the apostle to the apostles.

This title is not poetic flattery. It acknowledges that Mary was entrusted with a message before the others. She was sent, which is what the word "apostle" means. In some strands of early Christian tradition, this was taken seriously. But as the institutional church developed, her position was gradually minimized. Her leadership was reinterpreted, her voice absorbed into more acceptable roles—penitent, mourner, helper.

Yet the historical memory of her as apostle never entirely disappeared. It resurfaced in apocryphal texts like the Gospel of Mary, where she is not only a witness but a teacher—someone who not only receives a vision but interprets it. Her authority in that text is not dependent on institutional backing. It arises from experience, from presence, from understanding.

Alongside this literal and historical reading, another dimension has emerged—one that sees Mary as an archetype rather than simply a figure of the past. In this view, she is not only a woman who lived, but a symbol that continues to live in us. She becomes the embodiment of inner knowing, of sacred receptivity, of the transformative power of the soul. She is the one who does not forget, who sees beyond appearances, who holds the space between doubt and revelation.

Seeing Mary as archetype does not erase her humanity. On the contrary, it amplifies her meaning, allowing her to speak not only as an individual, but as a reflection of something larger: the human capacity for gnosis, for spiritual clarity, for remembering what has been hidden. In this role, Mary becomes a guide—not only to what happened, but to what is always happening within us.

These two readings—apostle and archetype—are not mutually exclusive. They operate on different levels. One is rooted in historical continuity, the other in symbolic resonance. One looks to Mary as a real person with a story in time; the other sees her as a timeless figure who continues to appear wherever someone dares to trust their inner vision.

Each has its value. The historical reading gives weight to her role in the movement around Jesus. It affirms her presence, her voice, her importance in the early formation of the Christian path. It challenges the long-standing erasure of women in leadership. It insists that her name belongs in the record not as a footnote, but as a foundational presence.

The archetypal reading, on the other hand, opens space for those who seek a spiritual mirror. It allows Mary to be not only remembered, but re-encountered. In her, we can find the courage to listen differently, to speak from silence, to trust what has no external validation but burns with internal truth.

One need not choose between the two. In fact, holding both perspectives may be the most honest way to engage her story. She may very well have been a real woman, entrusted with a message, misunderstood by her peers, and forgotten by history. And she may also be more than that—a living image of wisdom that endures, reappearing wherever the voice of the soul is honored over the voice of convention.

In the Gospel of Mary, these dimensions overlap. She is a person in the room—grieving, speaking, holding space. But she is also more than a disciple. She carries a message from the Savior that no one else heard. She interprets it without hesitation. She remains standing when the others collapse in fear. Her authority is not formal, but it is undeniable.

Seeing Mary as both apostle and archetype allows us to approach her with humility and depth. We can honor the path she walked, while also recognizing the path she still opens in us. She does not ask for devotion. She offers presence. And in that presence, we begin to remember—who she was, who we are, and what wisdom still waits to rise where it was once denied.

4.5 THE CONFLICT WITH PETER AND THE DEBATE OVER HER AUTHORITY

The Gospel of Mary does not end with consensus. It ends with conflict—not between good and evil, but between two disciples who both followed Jesus, and yet interpret his message very differently. At the center of this tension stands Mary Magdalene, not just as the bearer of a vision, but as the subject of doubt.

After Mary shares the soul's ascent and the teaching she received privately from the Savior, Peter challenges her. His words are abrupt and suspicious: "Did he really speak with a woman in private and not openly to us? Are we to turn and all listen to her? Did he prefer her to us?" These questions are rhetorical, even accusatory. They expose more than skepticism—they reveal a deep discomfort with the idea that a woman might have been entrusted with sacred knowledge that the others were not.

Peter's reaction is not merely personal. He represents a strand of early Christian leadership that would later become dominant—one focused on public authority, visible hierarchy, and male leadership. In that context, Mary's role is not just inconvenient—it's subversive. If what she says is true, then the very structure of authority is up for debate.

Mary doesn't argue. She weeps. Her tears are not weakness—they are a human response to being doubted for speaking from the heart. But before silence can swallow the moment, Levi intervenes. He defends Mary, pointing out that if the Savior loved her more than the others—as the text implies—then her voice should be honored, not dismissed. He urges them to "clothe yourselves with the perfect Human" and go out to preach the good news, not in competition, but in harmony.

This moment is crucial. It suggests that disagreement was part of the early Christian experience. The gospel doesn't present an idealized unity—it shows us the reality of a community grappling with questions of inclusion, voice, and legitimacy.

The debate over Mary's authority is more than a historical detail. It is a mirror held up to the church, to society, and to all of us. It asks: Who gets to speak? Who gets to be believed? And what might we lose when we silence the voices that don't fit the mold?

5 - THE THEOLOGICAL AND PHILOSOPHICAL THEMES

5.1 WHAT SPIRITUAL MESSAGE DOES THIS TEXT OFFER?

At its core, the Gospel of Mary is not a book of rules. It doesn't offer commandments, rituals, or institutional frameworks. Instead, it offers something more intimate and, in some ways, more demanding: a spiritual path rooted in self-knowledge, inner peace, and the liberation of the soul from illusion.

Unlike the canonical gospels, where salvation is often tied to belief, baptism, or obedience, the Gospel of Mary presents a vision in which salvation comes through awakening—a deep recognition of the truth already present within us. Jesus does not point outward toward laws or priests. He points inward. "The Son of Humanity is within you," he says. Not above. Not beyond. But within.

This inner turn is the gospel's boldest claim. It suggests that we are not passive recipients of grace, but active participants in our own liberation. The soul's journey, as described in Mary's vision, is a process of peeling away the layers of fear, desire, ignorance, and violence that keep us bound. As each force confronts the soul, it must answer not with argument, but with clarity. It must know itself—and in that knowing, it becomes free.

But the gospel's message is not just mystical. It is also deeply practical. When the disciples fall into fear after Jesus' departure, Mary doesn't scold or preach. She reminds them of what they already know. "Let us rather praise his greatness," she says, "for he has prepared us." Her words are a spiritual anchor. They call us back to what we've heard but may have forgotten: that fear is not the final word.

Perhaps that's the most powerful message this text offers: you are already prepared. The truth is not hidden in distant heavens or locked behind sacred institutions. It lives in your capacity to remember, to trust, and to see with new eyes.

The Gospel of Mary doesn't demand allegiance. It extends an invitation—one that begins with stillness and leads, step by step, toward freedom.

5.2 THE CONCEPT OF INNER KNOWLEDGE (GNOSIS) AS THE PATH TO SALVATION

One of the most radical ideas in the Gospel of Mary is that salvation doesn't come from outside—from rules, miracles, or even divine intervention. It comes from within, through a process the ancient world called gnosis, a Greek word meaning "knowledge." But not just any knowledge. We're not talking about facts or doctrines. This is personal, transformative insight—the kind that shifts your entire way of seeing.

The Jesus of this gospel doesn't urge his followers to follow a set of laws. He invites them to discover who they truly are beneath the noise of fear, expectation, and social conditioning. The real work is not about performing the right rituals or joining the right group.

It's about remembering—remembering the soul's origin, its nature, and its path back to wholeness.

Mary's vision paints this beautifully. The soul doesn't win its freedom by force. It moves upward by recognizing what it is not. "I saw you, but you did not see me," it says to one of the powers trying to hold it back. This isn't arrogance—it's clarity. The soul has seen through the illusion. It no longer confuses itself with desire or anger or ignorance. And in that recognition, it slips free.

This inward path doesn't deny suffering. It doesn't pretend that life is easy or that answers are obvious. But it suggests that liberation is possible—not by avoiding struggle, but by facing it with awareness. Each force the soul encounters mirrors something we know: the pull of craving, the fog of confusion, the sting of fear. The journey isn't abstract—it's the journey of being human.

What's so moving about this message is its trust in the reader. The Gospel of Mary doesn't preach at us. It assumes we're capable of seeing truth for ourselves, if we're willing to look. It doesn't build walls between "us" and "them," between the saved and the lost. Instead, it offers a quiet confidence: that the divine spark is already inside, waiting to be uncovered.

This makes gnosis less a destination and more a way of being—a kind of sacred attention. To live with gnosis is to move through the world awake, able to name what is real and let go of what is false. It's not about escaping life, but engaging it more fully, without getting trapped by appearances.

For readers today, this may feel both ancient and oddly modern. In a time when many are disillusioned with institutions but still hungry for meaning, the Gospel of Mary whispers something gentle yet powerful: you are not broken. You are not far. The truth you're looking for may already be inside you, quiet but waiting.

5.3 A DIFFERENT UNDERSTANDING OF SIN AND REDEMPTION COMPARED TO CANONICAL GOSPELS

If there's one moment in the Gospel of Mary that truly surprises readers familiar with traditional Christian teachings, it's when Jesus says, plainly: "There is no sin." The sentence arrives without buildup, without explanation. It stops you cold. Not because it denies human pain or wrongdoing, but because it reframes them entirely.

In most Christian traditions, sin is a central idea—something to be confessed, forgiven, cleansed. It's often tied to rules: break them, and you fall; obey them, and you're saved. But here, sin is not presented as a violation of divine law. Instead, it's described as a result of confusion—a misunderstanding of who we are and what reality truly is.

This gospel suggests that what we call sin arises when we forget our origin, when we identify more with our ego, our fears, or our desires than with the truth at our core. In other words, sin is not a stain on the soul—it's a veil over the eyes. And the path to healing isn't punishment or penance—it's clarity.

That's why the solution isn't sacrifice or atonement. It's awakening. Once we remember the truth—once we recognize that we are not defined by anger, jealousy, or fear—we begin to live differently. Not because someone tells us how to behave, but because our perception shifts. We no longer act out of fear or grasping, because we see where those roads lead.

It's a more compassionate view of the human condition. Instead of labeling people as sinners in need of rescue, the Gospel of Mary sees them as souls in need of remembrance. And redemption, then, becomes not a gift granted from outside, but a light that re-emerges from within.

This doesn't make the gospel naïve. It takes seriously the real harm we cause ourselves and others. But it invites us to heal not through guilt, but through insight. And in doing so, it reclaims something many have lost in their spiritual journeys: the idea that we are not inherently flawed, but inherently unfinished—capable of growth, return, and restoration.

5.4 SPIRITUAL FREEDOM AS THE CORE MESSAGE OF THE TEXT

Beneath every conversation, vision, and conflict in the Gospel of Mary, one idea pulses quietly but steadily: freedom. Not the kind granted by rulers or institutions, but a deep, spiritual freedom—freedom from fear, from illusion, from the false self we carry like a mask.

This freedom isn't promised as a reward. It's described as something already accessible, something we forgot rather than lost. The gospel's teachings guide us not toward a distant paradise, but toward a state of liberation available in the present moment, if we can shed the layers that keep us bound.

The soul's journey, as recounted by Mary, is really a process of letting go. Each barrier it encounters—Desire, Ignorance, Wrath—represents a force that claims control over the soul. But with each confrontation, the soul responds not by fighting, but by remembering what it is. It breaks free not through struggle, but through clarity.

This idea reframes what it means to be spiritual. It's not about striving, proving, or earning favor. It's about awakening to what's already true. In that sense, the Gospel of Mary aligns with wisdom traditions across cultures: the idea that the sacred is not far away, but hidden in plain sight—beneath distraction, fear, and noise.

What's especially powerful is how this freedom connects to inner peace. When the disciples panic after Jesus leaves, Mary reminds them of his words: "Let no one lead you astray, saying, 'Lo here!' or 'Lo there!' For the Son of Humanity is within you." It's a simple but seismic message. The truth isn't somewhere else. You don't have to chase it. You only have to stop running.

In this gospel, spiritual freedom isn't just a possibility—it's a birthright. And yet, it asks something of us. It asks for honesty, the courage to face ourselves without judgment, and the willingness to release the identities we cling to. That may be the hardest part of all. But it is also the beginning of peace.

5.5 OTHER GOSPELS, OTHER VOICES

The Gospel of Mary is powerful in its solitude—but it was never truly alone. In the early centuries of Christianity, dozens of writings emerged alongside what would later become the New Testament. Some offered alternative teachings of Jesus. Others explored mystical experiences, visions, or philosophical interpretations of salvation. Many were eventually labeled "apocryphal"—a word that means "hidden" or "obscure"—but these texts were not necessarily rejected at first. In fact, they were copied, shared, and studied in diverse Christian communities across the ancient world.

What unites many of these writings is a shared focus on inner knowledge, the liberation of the soul, and a direct relationship with the divine—themes echoed throughout the Gospel of Mary. While each text has its own voice, they often circle the same spiritual questions: What does it mean to be truly human?

THE THEOLOGICAL AND PHILOSOPHICAL THEMES

What is the nature of truth? How do we awaken to something greater than ourselves?

Now, we explore six such texts—some well-known, others less familiar. We begin with the Gospel of Thomas, a collection of Jesus' sayings that emphasizes personal insight over institutional belief. Then we turn to the Gospel of Philip, where love and mystery shape the understanding of spiritual union. The Gospel of Judas presents a radically different vision of betrayal and divine knowledge, challenging the narrative we thought we knew. Beyond these three more commonly referenced texts, we include two lesser-known writings: Pistis Sophia, a complex revelation text that explores the feminine divine and the soul's long journey toward the Light, and the Gospel of Truth, a poetic meditation on memory, reconciliation, and the healing of ignorance.

As we listen to these voices, the Gospel of Mary takes on new dimension. It resonates with their themes, but also stands apart. Mary's gospel is uniquely intimate—less cosmic than Pistis Sophia, less cryptic than Thomas, more emotionally grounded than Judas. It doesn't dazzle with myth or overwhelm with doctrine. It speaks in a quiet, steady voice. These comparisons are not about ranking or validation. They are about understanding the broader spiritual conversation happening in the early centuries of Christianity. And in that conversation, Mary's voice remains unforgettable—not because it shouts, but because it still whispers with clarity.

The Gospel of Thomas

There is something disarming about the Gospel of Thomas. It doesn't tell a story. There are no miracles, no crucifixion, no resurrection. Instead, we are given a series of sayings—short, sometimes cryptic, sometimes piercing in their simplicity. One follows another like stepping stones through a quiet, mysterious garden. And as you walk through them, something shifts: you don't feel you're learning about Jesus—you feel you're being spoken to directly.

The Gospel of Thomas opens with a promise: "Whoever finds the meaning of these words will not taste death." That line alone tells you what this text is about—not doctrine, but discovery. It doesn't ask you to believe. It asks you to see. Like the Gospel of Mary, Thomas emphasizes a form of knowledge that isn't external or inherited. It's internal, personal, and awakening. Jesus, in this gospel, does not save by dying—he teaches by provoking the mind and heart. He speaks in paradox, urging the listener to look past appearances. "If you bring forth what is within you, what you bring forth will save you." That message could sit just as easily in Mary's gospel.

But there are differences, too. Thomas is more elusive. The sayings don't follow a logical structure or narrative arc. Some feel like riddles. Others are tender, even startling. In one passage, Jesus says, "Split a piece of wood; I am there. Lift a stone, and you will find me there." It's a reminder that the divine is not distant, but hidden in plain sight—in the ordinary, in the overlooked.

Where the Gospel of Mary gives us a glimpse of intimacy—Mary's tears, her vision, her conflict with Peter—Thomas remains impersonal. We don't see characters. We don't see struggle. What we're given instead is a mirror. The sayings are spare, but they reflect us back to ourselves. They ask: What do you truly know? What are you ready to recognize?

Both texts share a sense of urgency without fear. There is no threat of damnation in Thomas, just as there is none in Mary. What drives both is the sense that we are asleep, and that something within us is waiting to awaken. That awakening isn't granted by ritual or authority—it happens when we begin to see differently. In reading Thomas, you may not understand every saying. But you may feel something else: a presence. Not loud, not demanding—just there. Like a teacher who doesn't explain, but stands quietly by as you begin to understand for yourself.

In that way, Thomas and Mary walk parallel paths. They are both gospels of the soul—less concerned with history, more concerned with memory. Not the kind of memory that recalls facts, but the kind that remembers who you really are.

The Gospel of Philip

The Gospel of Philip is a strange and beautiful text. Part mystical meditation, part theological reflection, it comes to us in fragmented form—lines missing, transitions unclear. And yet, through the gaps, something powerful emerges: a deep fascination with union, intimacy, and the mysterious bond between Jesus and Mary Magdalene.

Unlike the Gospel of Mary, which gives us dialogue and vision, Philip offers brief poetic passages that often feel like whispers from another world. Some are esoteric, others almost tender. One of its most well-known lines reads: "The Savior loved her more than all the disciples and used to kiss her often on the mouth." That single sentence has stirred centuries of speculation—but perhaps we miss the point if we read it only as gossip or scandal. The word that stands out more than "kiss" is "loved." In Philip, love is not mere affection—it is recognition. The kiss, in gnostic symbolism, was often a sign of the transmission of knowledge or spirit. In this light, the relationship between Jesus and Mary is not romantic in the modern sense—it's sacramental, sacred, and spiritually equal.

The Gospel of Philip repeatedly uses the word "companion" to describe Mary Magdalene. The Greek word may be koinōnos—a term that implies not just partnership, but shared purpose, shared life. In a world where women were often named only in relation to men, here is a woman named as equal in purpose. That alone is revolutionary. Like the Gospel of Mary, Philip offers a vision of salvation that is deeply internal.

It speaks of wholeness, of reuniting the scattered parts of the soul. It explores the idea that what is broken in us can be made whole not through law or fear, but through union—within ourselves, with the divine, and with others.

There is also a recurring theme of what is hidden becoming visible. The bridal chamber, often referenced in the text, is not just a metaphor for intimacy—it is a place where opposites are reconciled: male and female, body and spirit, knowledge and mystery. In this sense, Mary represents not just a woman, but a principle of spiritual integration.

Yet, for all its complexity, Philip also feels incomplete. It doesn't explain itself. It leaves space for silence, ambiguity, and personal interpretation. This makes it a natural companion to the Gospel of Mary, which also invites us not to analyze, but to listen inwardly.

Together, these two gospels—Mary and Philip—create a dialogue. One speaks through vision, the other through symbolism. One presents Mary as teacher and leader; the other as beloved and vessel of wisdom. Both challenge us to see that authority doesn't always look like power. Sometimes, it looks like love. Like trust. Like quiet presence. In Philip, Mary is not the center of the narrative—but she is its key. And that, perhaps, is the most lasting image: not of a woman on the margins, but of a companion who holds a truth the world forgot to remember.

The Gospel of Judas

Of all the apocryphal gospels, few have sparked as much controversy—and fascination—as the Gospel of Judas. Its very title is unsettling. We know Judas Iscariot as the traitor, the one who handed Jesus over to death. To hear that his gospel exists, and that it tells a different story, feels like a provocation.

And it is. But not in the way we might think. This text, discovered in a Coptic manuscript in the 1970s and made widely known in the early 2000s, presents Judas not as a villain, but as a chosen one. In this gospel, Jesus shares secret knowledge with Judas alone. He tells him that the other disciples misunderstand his message. He tells him that his "betrayal" is not a failure, but a necessary act that will release the spirit from the body. Judas, in this vision, is the only one who truly understands—and the only one willing to bear the cost of that understanding.

Whether we take this literally or symbolically, the Gospel of Judas confronts us with a central idea: that truth is not always where we expect to find it. And sometimes, those labeled as outsiders or enemies carry a wisdom that others overlook or reject. Like the Gospel of Mary, Judas is part of a tradition that values inner knowledge over external authority. In both texts, we see tension between the one who receives hidden insight and the rest of the group. In Mary's gospel, Peter challenges her authority. In Judas's, the other disciples are portrayed as unable to grasp the deeper truths Jesus is offering.

But the tone is quite different. Where Mary is quiet, intimate, and healing, Judas is dramatic, cosmic, even disturbing. It speaks of aeons, stars, and divine realms, and uses the language of myth to describe spiritual realities. It feels less like a gospel and more like a theological vision written in code.

Still, at its core is a question that echoes through all the apocryphal texts: Who really understood Jesus? And perhaps more importantly: Who gets to tell the story?

The Gospel of Judas doesn't give us Mary Magdalene. In fact, it offers almost no female presence at all. But it does offer a profound critique of religious systems that prioritize ritual, appearance, or groupthink over spiritual perception. Judas, like Mary in her gospel, is the one who steps outside the group— misunderstood, maligned, and ultimately cast out. This does not mean the two gospels are saying the same thing. But they both challenge the idea that spiritual truth is defined by consensus. They both elevate the figure who dares to listen differently— and to act from that listening.

Reading the Gospel of Judas can be uncomfortable. It overturns one of the most familiar narratives in Christian tradition. But discomfort can also be a teacher. Like Mary's voice, Judas's challenges us to question what we've inherited, to look again, and to wonder what else might be hidden in plain sight.

Pistis Sophia

Among the many texts recovered from early Christian and gnostic sources, Pistis Sophia stands out as one of the most complex—and most mystical. At over three hundred pages in translation, it is far longer than most apocryphal writings and feels more like a spiritual treatise than a gospel. It takes the form of a dialogue between Jesus and his disciples—especially Mary Magdalene—after the resurrection, and it centers on a mysterious figure named Sophia, the embodiment of divine wisdom.

The word "Sophia" is Greek for "wisdom," and she appears in both Jewish and Christian traditions, often personified as a feminine presence. In Pistis Sophia, she is more than a symbol. She is a being who has fallen from the higher realms and now longs to return to the Light. But her journey is hard. She is attacked by dark powers, betrayed by those she trusted, and must plead for help again and again. Each time, she is raised a little higher, but the ascent is slow, painful, and filled with longing.

For many readers, Sophia's story feels deeply human. It is the story of the soul that has lost its way, that has forgotten its origin, and that must remember, through suffering and persistence, who it truly is. There is no quick salvation here. No miracle fixes everything. The path back to wholeness is layered, mysterious, and deeply emotional.

What makes this text especially significant in relation to the Gospel of Mary is Mary's role within it. In Pistis Sophia, Mary Magdalene is not a silent witness—she is the one who speaks the most. Again and again, she asks questions, offers interpretations, and responds to Jesus' teachings. She is presented as the most perceptive of the disciples, the one who understands the hidden meanings behind the revelations.

The tone of the dialogue between Jesus and Mary here is formal but intimate. He often praises her insight. She shows no hesitation in stepping forward. This consistent pattern reinforces the image of Mary as a bearer of wisdom, a living counterpart to Sophia herself.

While Pistis Sophia is filled with elaborate cosmology—layers of heavens, ranks of beings, cycles of descent and ascent—it also contains moments of profound psychological insight. Sophia's laments, scattered throughout the text, read almost like psalms. They are poems of sorrow, repentance, and hope. In her, we can see the human soul in all its complexity: lost, yearning, resilient. Where the Gospel of Mary is quiet and grounded, Pistis Sophia is vast and mythic. One speaks in personal experience, the other in celestial drama. And yet, they meet in the same heart: both offer a vision of the feminine as wise, powerful, and essential to the path of return.

In a tradition that often silenced or sidelined women, these two texts—different as they are—preserve voices that refuse to disappear. Sophia, the fallen wisdom; Mary, the faithful seeker. One ascends through the stars. The other speaks from the heart. And together, they remind us that truth is not only told in dogma—but also in longing, in insight, and in the courage to speak what others forget to hear.

The Gospel of Truth

The Gospel of Truth reads like a meditation. It doesn't tell a story, nor does it recount events or name specific disciples. Instead, it speaks in flowing, poetic language about truth, ignorance, memory, and love. It's not so much a gospel about Jesus as it is a gospel from a deep place of spiritual insight—one that sees the human condition not as sinful, but as forgetful.

At the heart of this text is the idea that we suffer not because we are bad or broken, but because we have forgotten who we are and where we come from. Salvation, then, is not a transaction—it is a process of remembering. As the text puts it: "Ignorance brought about anguish and terror. And the anguish grew solid like a fog, so that no one could see." And yet, in this fog, something stirs. The Savior comes not to punish, but to remind.

Unlike the Gospel of Judas or Pistis Sophia, this text contains no complex cosmology. There are no aeons or multiple layers of heavens. Instead, it focuses on the psychological and spiritual reality of disconnection—and the deep joy of returning to the truth. In a world built on fear and forgetting, love becomes the force that calls us home.

The Gospel of Truth doesn't name Mary Magdalene, but its spirit resonates closely with hers. The focus on inner knowing, on awakening from confusion, and on the healing power of peace echoes the voice we hear in the Gospel of Mary. Both texts suggest that truth is not taught—it is revealed, and what is revealed is something we already carry inside us.

What's striking in the Gospel of Truth is its tenderness. There is no sense of condemnation. Even those who are lost in illusion are not blamed—they are simply sleeping. And the goal is not control, but reunion. It's a message that feels deeply compatible with Mary's own gospel, where sin is defined not as offense, but as misunderstanding. In this sense, the Gospel of Truth offers a kind of quiet bridge—between the mystical language of gnostic cosmology and the clear, personal wisdom of the Gospel of Mary. It doesn't contradict other texts—it softens them. It brings light to the darker visions, and reminds us that, beneath all seeking, there is love waiting to be remembered.

Among all these voices— esoteric, symbolic, revolutionary— Mary's remains the most human.

She does not speak in riddles or cosmic visions. She speaks from experience: from pain, from presence, from love. Hers is not the voice of a doctrine, but of a person who has seen, remembered, and dares to speak. And perhaps that is why, after all the mysteries and myths, it is her voice that stays with us the longest.

6 – MAGDALENE AND SOPHIA: ECHOES OF THE DIVINE FEMININE

6.1 WISDOM IN EXILE: SOPHIA IN THE BIBLICAL AND GNOSTIC TRADITIONS

Long before Mary Magdalene was remembered as a voice of wisdom and insight, there was Sophia—the personification of divine wisdom. Her presence runs quietly through ancient texts, sometimes speaking clearly, sometimes hidden in symbol. She is both near and distant, exalted and forgotten. And always, she is calling us to remember something we've lost.

In the Hebrew Scriptures, Sophia (in Hebrew Chokhmah, in Greek Sophia) is not an idea, but a figure. In Proverbs, she stands at the crossroads, calling out to those who pass by: "To you, O people, I call out; I raise my voice to all mankind." She is described as present before creation, as one who "was beside Him like a master worker", rejoicing in the world, delighting in humanity. In the Book of Wisdom and Sirach, she is radiant, subtle, and powerful—yet too often rejected.

But it is in the gnostic writings, especially those discovered at Nag Hammadi, that Sophia takes on a dramatic role. She becomes not just a presence, but a story—one of light, fall, struggle, and return. In texts like Pistis Sophia, she descends from the higher realms in search of something good, but is trapped in darkness. Betrayed by lesser powers, she is stripped of her light and cries out for help. Again and again, she prays for deliverance. Her voice is lament, longing, and persistent faith.

Sophia is not punished for rebellion. She is wounded for seeking. And that is what makes her so profoundly human. Her journey is not about sin—it's about separation. Not about guilt, but about forgetting the way home. In many of these texts, Sophia is not rescued instantly. Her return to the Light is gradual, supported by the compassion of the divine and her own remembrance. She becomes a model for the soul—not as sinner, but as seeker. A figure who embodies both divine presence and human struggle.

What's striking is how Sophia is portrayed not as passive, but as powerful. Her fall shakes the cosmos. Her cry moves the heavens. And her restoration brings balance. She is not a background figure in salvation. She is part of its unfolding.

Yet, despite her central role, Sophia was largely erased from official theology. Her name disappeared from the creeds. Her wisdom was reframed as male Logos. Her cries were silenced, her story forgotten. And yet—like Mary—she persists. She lingers in symbols, returns in forgotten texts, and speaks again in those who listen. Sophia's story, like Mary's, reminds us that wisdom was never lost—it was only exiled. And now, it returns.

6.2 A MIRROR IN MAGDALENE: PARALLELS BETWEEN TWO SILENCED VOICES

Sophia and Magdalene never meet in the texts—not directly. One belongs to a cosmic drama of fall and return, the other to a quiet gospel of peace and presence. And yet, when we listen closely, the resonance between them is unmistakable. They speak with different voices, from different traditions, but they both carry the same sacred burden: a wisdom the world was not ready to hear.

Sophia falls from the fullness of divine Light into chaos, her light scattered, her voice crying out. Mary, in her gospel, doesn't fall—but she stands in a world that doubts her, questions her authority, and challenges her memory of what she saw and heard. Sophia is betrayed by false powers. Mary is interrupted by Peter.

Both are voices of insight, both are disbelieved not because they are unclear, but because they are inconvenient. They disrupt the order. They speak truths that others would rather keep hidden. In that sense, they are sisters across time—each a mirror for the other.

Sophia represents the soul in exile, stripped of clarity, yet still longing for return. Mary represents the soul that remembers, even when surrounded by doubt. Sophia pleads; Mary speaks. Sophia weeps; Mary comforts. And both are answered—not with silence, but with recognition.

What they share is not only marginalization. They also share a particular kind of knowing—not logical, not institutional, but deep, lived, interior. Sophia's wisdom is ancient, radiant, and poetic. Mary's is grounded, embodied, and quietly unwavering. They show us that knowledge does not always arrive through formal teaching. Sometimes it emerges through presence, through listening, through the willingness to see what others cannot.

In both figures, we encounter not just "the feminine," but the sacred feminine—a wisdom that is relational rather than dominant, intuitive rather than imposed, born not of conquest but of remembering. This is not about gender as biology or power dynamic. It is about a mode of insight the early church often feared: a voice that doesn't obey, but reveals.

Their silencing is not accidental. It reflects the tension at the heart of spiritual tradition: between control and revelation, between the need for order and the risk of awakening. Sophia is stripped of her light, Mary of her credibility. And yet both continue to speak, not through authority granted, but through truth remembered.

Seeing Mary Magdalene through the lens of Sophia doesn't reduce her—it elevates the scope of her role. She is not only a disciple or companion. She is a bearer of Wisdom, the echo of something far older than her own name.

When Sophia weeps, Mary answers. When Mary is questioned, Sophia rises. And between the two, a hidden lineage comes to light—one that runs beneath the surface of the tradition, waiting for those who have ears to hear.

6.3 THE RETURN OF THE SACRED FEMININE

Over the past century, and especially in recent decades, there has been a quiet yet steady reawakening of interest in what many call the sacred feminine. This movement has not come from institutions or doctrines, but from the personal and often intimate search for something that has long been missing—a dimension of spirituality that honors intuition, embodiment, compassion, and deep relational knowing. Across many paths and traditions, people have begun to recognize that wisdom has not always been transmitted in abstract teachings or hierarchical structures, but also in the gentler rhythms of listening, remembering, and presence.

In this context, figures like Mary Magdalene and Sophia have found their voices again—not only as historical or mythic symbols, but as spiritual presences that continue to resonate. Their reemergence is not the result of ideological reaction or romantic projection, but a response to a deeper hunger for balance. For centuries, dominant religious traditions have leaned heavily toward transcendence, discipline, and authority—qualities often coded as masculine—while marginalizing those aspects of experience that are cyclical, tender, embodied, and mysterious. What is now being sought is not a reversal of that imbalance, but a quiet integration.

The sacred feminine is not a slogan or a system. It is the return of something that was always there, waiting to be seen again. It manifests not in grand gestures, but in the way we come to trust inner movements of the heart, in the way we make space for vulnerability, in the way silence becomes a teacher rather than an absence to be filled. It speaks in art, in healing, in the reverence for the Earth, in the reclamation of stories that once were buried.

In recovering the figure of Mary Magdalene—not as a repentant sinner, but as a teacher and knower—we participate in this broader return. We restore not only a woman's name to the story, but a mode of wisdom that does not seek to dominate, only to reveal. Her presence, like that of Sophia, invites a different posture: one of openness rather than certainty, of receptivity rather than defense. And perhaps that is where the sacred feminine lives most fully—not in contrast to what has come before, but alongside it, completing what was never meant to be divided.

6.4 KNOWLEDGE AS REUNION, NOT CONTROL

In many of the texts where figures like Mary Magdalene or Sophia appear, knowledge is not presented as something to be mastered or defended. It is not a system, a doctrine, or a boundary to be guarded. Rather, it is something remembered—something that rises slowly, like light returning after a long night. It is not about having the right answers, but about seeing again what had been forgotten.

The tradition from which the Gospel of Mary emerges does not treat knowledge as a possession. It does not come through authority, status, or ritual, but through inner clarity and personal awakening. This knowledge does not separate—it reconnects. It helps the soul recognize its own origin, and in doing so, it restores a sense of belonging that had been lost. It is not power in the usual sense. It does not control, but gently undoes what has kept us bound.

In this light, the figure of Mary becomes more than a disciple—she becomes a model of how knowing can be quiet, grounded, and deeply relational. Her understanding is not loud or argumentative. It is stable, rooted in experience, and offered without force. She does not demand to be heard, but when she speaks, something essential returns to the circle. Her voice brings the others back to peace. That is what true knowledge does—it brings rest, not conflict.

The same can be said of Sophia. Her knowledge is not a triumph. It is a homecoming. Her journey through darkness is not a quest for control, but a longing to return to wholeness. She rises not by conquering the powers that trapped her, but by remembering who she is and where she belongs. Her restoration is not imposed from outside. It happens gradually, through recognition and support. In both figures, we find a vision of knowledge that feels less like an achievement and more like a return. It is humble, steady, and often invisible. And perhaps that is why it has been overlooked for so long—because it doesn't seek the spotlight. It simply restores what was always there.

In Mary and Sophia, two forgotten figures begin to speak again—not to impose a new order, but to remind us of what has been quietly waiting beneath the surface all along. Their wisdom is not distant or abstract; it is rooted in the human experience of exile, return, silence, and speech. In their stories, we don't find heroes or hierarchies—we find echoes of our own searching. And in their voices, calm and unwavering, something of the sacred becomes visible again: not as a power to be claimed, but as a presence to be received.

7 – WHY WAS THE GOSPEL OF MARY EXCLUDED?

7.1 WHY WAS THIS GOSPEL NOT INCLUDED IN THE NEW TESTAMENT?

To understand why the Gospel of Mary never found a place in the New Testament, we have to remember that the Bible as we know it didn't fall from the sky, fully formed. It was shaped—over centuries—by a mix of theology, tradition, politics, and power. In the earliest days of Christianity, there was no single canon, no agreed-upon list of "official" books. There were many gospels, letters, and teachings circulating among diverse communities, each with its own understanding of who Jesus was and what his message meant.

The Gospel of Mary was likely written in the second century, at a time when Christian thought was still wide open and diverse. Some groups emphasized Jewish law and continuity; others leaned into mystical teachings, radical ethics, or personal revelation. The version of Christianity that eventually became "orthodox" was not the only one—it just became the most dominant.

That dominance began to solidify in the late second and third centuries, when church leaders started identifying which texts aligned with what they saw as the true faith. Criteria included apostolic authorship, widespread use in liturgy, and theological compatibility. But even these standards were applied inconsistently. Debates over what belonged in the canon raged for generations. Some books we now consider central—like Revelation or James—were hotly contested. Others, like the

Shepherd of Hermas or 1 Clement, were beloved and widely read, but ultimately excluded.

So where does that leave the Gospel of Mary?

It failed several of the early "tests." First, it wasn't clearly attributed to one of the Twelve Apostles, and the idea that Mary Magdalene could be considered an authoritative teacher was controversial—especially as male leadership began to dominate church structures. Second, its theology clashed with emerging orthodox doctrines, especially on sin, salvation, and authority. The gospel's emphasis on inner knowledge, the soul's journey, and the rejection of legalistic religion likely felt too "gnostic" for the mainstream. Even though it doesn't promote a full Gnostic cosmology, its tone was enough to raise suspicions.

But perhaps most threatening of all was its central character. A woman, receiving direct revelation from Jesus, correcting the disciples, and being affirmed as worthy? In an age when ecclesiastical roles were being formalized and power was being centralized, that was a message too disruptive to tolerate.

Over time, the text simply fell out of circulation. Not banned, not burned—just ignored. Manuscripts weren't copied. Scribes moved on. And like many other early Christian writings that didn't make the cut, it slipped into obscurity.

Its exclusion wasn't just about theology—it was about control. Which voices were allowed to define the faith? Which memories were preserved? The Gospel of Mary reminds us that the history of Christianity could have been written differently—and in some small way, it still is.

7.2 THE ROLE OF ORAL TRADITION AND MANUSCRIPT TRANSMISSION

In the early centuries of Christianity, oral tradition was the heartbeat of the faith. Before ink met parchment, stories of Jesus were passed from voice to voice, shared in homes, whispered in gatherings, and remembered in the hearts of those who heard them. The Gospel of Mary, like many early Christian texts, likely began this way—not as a fixed, written document, but as a living memory, shaped by the rhythm of speech and the intimacy of community.

This oral phase explains much about the diversity of early Christian thought. Communities in Alexandria, Antioch, Rome, and beyond preserved different stories, emphasized different teachings, and interpreted Jesus' words in their own contexts. When someone finally wrote down the Gospel of Mary—probably in Greek, sometime in the 2nd century—it was already a crystallization of something that had been told, pondered, and perhaps even debated for years.

But the leap from spoken word to manuscript didn't guarantee survival. Manuscript transmission was fragile, labor-intensive, and costly. Scribes chose what to copy based on what was valued in their community—and what aligned with accepted beliefs. Once a text fell out of favor, it was rarely recopied. Over time, forgotten manuscripts simply decayed or disappeared.

What we have of the Gospel of Mary survives thanks to a single Coptic copy from the 5th century, and two small Greek fragments. That's it. No church father quoted it. No major scriptorium preserved it. It survived against the odds, likely because someone, somewhere, found it worth copying—even as others turned away. This vulnerability reveals something deeper: that the shape of Christian memory wasn't just a matter of what was true, but of what was transmitted. And transmission was never neutral. It was shaped by faith, yes—but also by culture, bias, and the slow erosion of time.

7.3 THE ISSUE OF FEMALE AUTHORITY IN EARLY CHRISTIANITY

One of the quiet tensions running through the Gospel of Mary—and perhaps the reason it was so easily forgotten—is its unapologetic portrayal of a woman speaking with authority. In a time when church leadership was becoming increasingly male-dominated, this was more than unusual. It was unsettling.

Mary Magdalene is not shown as a helper, a background figure, or a passive listener. She teaches. She comforts. She interprets the words of Jesus. And when the male disciples fall into fear, it is she who reminds them of what the Savior taught. This wasn't just symbolic—it was revolutionary.

But by the second and third centuries, the role of women in Christian communities was becoming more limited. Early letters and writings—some of which made it into the New Testament—contain clues that women once held leadership roles: they hosted churches in their homes, led prayer, and in some cases, were even called apostles. Yet as the church grew in structure and began to mirror the social order of the Roman world, these spaces narrowed.

By the time church councils began defining orthodoxy, the idea of a woman as a primary teacher or visionary had become almost unthinkable. Texts like the Gospel of Mary, which placed a woman at the center of divine revelation, were quietly set aside. Not because they were theologically weak, but because they disrupted the narrative of who could speak on behalf of Christ.

The conflict with Peter in the gospel reflects this tension. His doubt isn't about Mary's message—it's about her right to deliver it. "Did he really speak with a woman… and not openly to us?" The question isn't just about content; it's about authority. Levi's defense of Mary reminds us that these questions weren't settled in the early church—they were active, debated, and unresolved.

That makes this gospel more than a spiritual text. It's also a historical document—a window into a moment when the shape of Christianity was still being formed, and the voices at the table were still in flux.

7.4 EARLY CRITIQUES OF MARY MAGDALENE IN PATRISTIC WRITINGS

While the Gospel of Mary elevates Mary Magdalene as a teacher and visionary, later Christian tradition did something very different: it reduced her. Over the centuries, Mary's image shifted from apostle and confidante to sinner and penitent—a transformation that began subtly, but gained momentum in the writings of the early Church Fathers.

In the canonical gospels, Mary Magdalene is portrayed with dignity. She is the first to witness the resurrection. Jesus calls her by name. Yet by the second century, ambiguity in her identity became fertile ground for reinterpretation. Several women named Mary appear in the gospels. One of them has demons cast out. Another is a sister of Lazarus. Still another is described as an anonymous woman who anoints Jesus' feet. The Church Fathers began to merge these figures, often with little textual support.

By the time of Pope Gregory the Great in the 6th century, this conflation became official. In a famous homily, he declared that Mary Magdalene was the same woman who had been a prostitute, had repented, and had anointed Christ. With this declaration, her legacy was effectively rewritten. No longer a leader, she became a cautionary tale of sin, repentance, and forgiveness.

Earlier Church Fathers, like Tertullian and Origen, didn't go quite so far, but they too contributed to a view of women as secondary in spiritual authority. While not all dismissed Mary Magdalene directly, the broader trend was clear: as Christian orthodoxy developed, so too did a more patriarchal theology—one that marginalized female figures, especially those who, like Mary, claimed intimacy with the divine.

The silence around the Gospel of Mary in patristic writings may not be accidental. Perhaps they never knew of the text. But it's also possible that its message—that a woman could be the bearer of inner truth—was simply too inconvenient to preserve.

And so, for centuries, Mary's voice faded—not because it lacked value, but because history was written by those who were not ready to hear her.

8 – HOW TO READ THIS TEXT

8.1 A LIVING TEXT, NOT A DEAD DOCUMENT

The text you're about to read is presented without line-by-line commentary. That's not an oversight—it's a deliberate choice. Rather than dissect the Gospel of Mary, we invite you to meet it as it is: fragmented, mysterious, and alive.

In the chapters before this, we've explored the historical background, the spiritual themes, and the powerful role Mary Magdalene plays in this gospel. We've laid a foundation. Now, it's your turn to enter the space the text creates—not as a scholar dissecting a specimen, but as a listener encountering a voice.

This gospel doesn't offer rigid doctrine. It doesn't follow a clear structure or narrative arc. Much of it is missing. And yet, that's part of its power. The gaps ask you to lean in. The silences invite you to pause. The message is not just in what's said, but in what remains unsaid.

We've chosen not to explain every line because this is a text that asks for reflection more than explanation. It speaks in images, gestures, and questions. It doesn't need to be solved. It needs to be heard.

So read slowly. Let it echo. And allow it to speak to you in its own strange, quiet way.

8.2 READING WITH OPENNESS AND WITHOUT DOGMA

The Gospel of Mary is not a text that demands belief—it invites presence. To read it well, you don't need theological training or religious affiliation. What you need is openness. A willingness to sit with mystery. A curiosity to let the words reach you before rushing to explain them.

This gospel doesn't try to convince or convert. It doesn't offer a system or a creed. Instead, it speaks gently of peace, knowledge, and the soul's journey. Some of it may resonate deeply. Other parts might confuse you. That's okay. It's not meant to be a puzzle with one correct solution.

Approach it more like poetry than theology. Let the imagery move you. Let the voice of Mary surprise you. Let the questions Jesus raises unsettle you in the best way. And allow yourself to feel—even when the meaning seems unclear. Sometimes what we feel in reading is more important than what we understand.

There's no wrong way to read this gospel. You can reflect on it slowly or let it wash over you in one sitting. Either way, it rewards quiet attention over certainty. This isn't about arriving at the right conclusion. It's about staying open to what might rise within you as you listen.

8.3 WHAT TO NOTICE WHILE READING

As you read the Gospel of Mary, you may notice that it doesn't follow the familiar rhythm of the canonical gospels. There are no parables, no miracles, no dramatic resurrection appearances. What it offers instead is quieter—and perhaps more intimate.

Pay attention to the tone. Jesus doesn't speak in commands. His words are calm, even gentle. He speaks of peace, not judgment. He doesn't tell the disciples what to believe; he tells them to find rest within themselves. That shift—from external rules to inner stillness—is central to this text.

Watch also for Mary's presence. She isn't just another follower. She remembers what others forget. She steps forward when the others fall into fear. Her authority doesn't come from status or appointment—it comes from insight. And yet, she's challenged for it. Peter's discomfort with her role mirrors the real-world tensions in the early Christian community, and perhaps in ours, too.

Another moment to notice is the soul's journey. When Mary recounts her vision, the imagery is symbolic but evocative. Desire, Ignorance, Wrath—these aren't just cosmic forces. They're parts of the human experience. The soul's dialogue with them feels strangely familiar. We know these voices. We wrestle with them, too.

You might also reflect on what's missing. The gospel begins mid-conversation and ends abruptly. We don't get every detail.

But that absence leaves space—space to wonder, to engage, to imagine. This isn't a complete map. It's a doorway.

So as you read, don't rush. Let the strangeness be part of the invitation. Ask yourself:
- What does this stir in me?
- Where do I feel resistance?
- What might this gospel be asking me to remember about myself?

8.4 A TEXT FOR SEEKERS

The Gospel of Mary is not a text that insists. It doesn't shout or demand to be followed. It waits quietly, offering itself to those who are still searching—seekers, not settlers.

If you come to this gospel looking for rules, you may be disappointed. But if you come with questions—with a longing for something deeper, something truer—it might feel like an unexpected home. This is a gospel for those who've felt out of place in rigid systems, who've sensed that spirituality must mean more than obedience.

You don't need to believe everything it says. You don't need to understand it all. What matters is your willingness to sit with it—to let its fragments speak, to let its silences breathe.

Some readers may approach this text as a historical curiosity. Others may find in it a voice that echoes something they've always known but never seen written down. Both are valid.

In the end, the Gospel of Mary doesn't close a conversation—it opens one. It invites you not to memorize or accept, but to explore. And perhaps, somewhere in its pages, you'll hear not just Mary's voice—but your own.

ADDITIONAL DIGITAL CONTENT

Scan the QR CODE NOW
to access all digital content!!!

+ EBOOK VERSION

3 EXTRA FANTASTIC RESOURCE
UNLOCK APOCRYPHIA'S SECRET

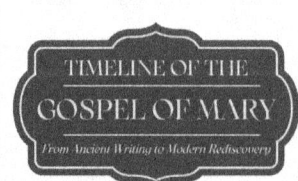

9 - THE GOSPEL OF MARY MAGDALENE

INTRODUCTION TO THE TEXT

What follows is the surviving portion of the Gospel of Mary, as preserved in a 5th-century Coptic manuscript, with two additional Greek fragments from earlier centuries. The text begins in the middle of a conversation and ends abruptly, with several pages missing. We have chosen to present it without commentary, so that you may encounter it directly—just as it has come down to us: incomplete, mysterious, and quietly powerful.

PAGES 1-6

The beginning of the Gospel of Mary is lost. The first six pages of the original manuscript—which probably included chapters 1 through 3—are missing entirely. What we have begins only on page 7, dropping us into the middle of a conversation already in progress. The opening context, whatever it once was, has been erased by time.

PAGE 7 - CH. 4

"Then will [matter] be [destroyed], or not?"

The Savior said, "Every nature, every form, every creature exists in and with each other, but they'll dissolve again into their own roots, because the nature of matter dissolves into its nature alone. Anyone who has ears to hear should hear!"

Peter said to him, "Since you've explained everything to us, tell us one more thing. What's the sin of the world?"

The Savior said, "Sin doesn't exist, but you're the ones who make sin when you act in accordance with the nature of adultery, which is called 'sin.' That's why the Good came among you, up to the things of every nature in order to restore it within its root."

Then he continued and said, "That's why you get sick and die, because [you love what tricks you. Anyone who] can understand should understand!

"Matter [gave birth to] a passion that has no image because it comes from what's contrary to nature. Then confusion arises in the whole body. That's why I told you to be content at heart. If you're discontented, find contentment in the presence of the various images of nature. Anyone who has ears to hear should hear!"

When the Blessed One said these things, he greeted them all and said, "Peace be with you! Acquire my peace. Be careful not to let anyone mislead you by saying, 'Look over here!' or 'Look over there!' Because the Son of Humanity exists within you. Follow him! Those who seek him will find him.

"Go then and preach the gospel about the kingdom. Don't lay down any rules beyond what I've given *you, nor make a law like the lawgiver, lest you be bound by it." When he said these things, he left.*

But they grieved and wept bitterly. They said, "How can we go up to the Gentiles to preach the gospel about the kingdom of the Son of Humanity? If they didn't spare him, why would they spare us?"

Then Mary arose and greeted them all. She said to her brothers (and sisters), "Don't weep and grieve or let your hearts be divided, because his grace will be with you all and will protect you. Rather we should praise his greatness because he's prepared us and made us Humans."

When Mary said these things, she turned their hearts [toward] the Good and they [started] to debate the words of [the Savior].

Peter said to Mary, "Sister, we know the Savior loved you more than all other women. Tell us the words of the Savior that you remember – the things which you know that we don't, and which we haven't heard."

In response Mary said, "I'll tell you what's hidden from you." So she started to tell them these words: "I," she said, "I saw the Lord in a vision and I said to him, 'Lord, I saw you in a vision today.'

"In response he said to me, 'You're blessed because you didn't waver at the sight of me. For where the mind is, there is the treasure.'

"I said to him, 'Lord, now does the one who sees the vision see it /in\ the soul /or\ in the spirit?'

"In response the Savior said, 'They don't see in the soul or in the spirit, but the mind which [exists] between the two is [what] sees the vision [and] it [that ...]

PAGES 11-14

The manuscript is also missing pages 11 through 14, which likely contained the conclusion of Chapter 5 and part of Chapter 6. These gaps leave a portion of Mary's vision incomplete, cutting off a part of the message that once connected more fully to the rest of the text.

PAGES 15 - CH. 8

"And Desire said, 'I didn't see you going down, but now I see you're going up. So why are you lying, since you belong to me?'

"In response the soul said, 'I saw you, but you didn't see me or know me. I was to you just a garment, and you didn't recognize me.' When it said these things, it left, rejoicing greatly.

"Again, it came to the third power, which is called 'Ignorance.' [It] interrogated the soul and [said], 'Where are you going? In wickedness you're bound. Since you're bound, don't judge!'

"[And] the soul said, 'Why do you judge me, since I haven't judged? I was bound, even though I haven't bound. They didn't recognize me, but I've recognized that everything will dissolve — both the things of the [earth] and the things of [heaven].'

"When the soul had overcome the third power, it went up and saw the fourth power, which took seven forms:

The first form is Darkness;

The second, Desire;

The third, Ignorance;

The fourth, Zeal for Death;

The fifth, the Kingdom of the Flesh;

The sixth, the Foolish 'Wisdom' of Flesh;
The seventh, the 'Wisdom' of Anger.

"These are the seven powers of Wrath.

"They ask the soul, 'Where do you come from, you murderer, and where are you going, conqueror of space?'

"In response the soul said, 'What binds me has been killed, what surrounds me has been overcome, my desire is gone, and ignorance has died. In a [world] I was released from a world, [and] in a type from a type which is above, and from the chain of forgetfulness which exists only for a time. From now on I'll receive the rest of the time of the season of the age in silence.'"

When Mary said these things, she fell silent because the Savior had spoken with her up to this point.

In response Andrew said to the brothers (and sisters), 'Say what you will about what she's said, I myself don't believe that the Savior said these things, because these teachings seem like different ideas."

In response Peter spoke out with the same concerns. He asked them concerning the Savior: "He didn't speak with a woman without our knowledge and not publicly with us, did he? Will we turn around and all listen to her? Did he prefer her to us?"

Then Mary wept and said to Peter, "My brother Peter, what are you thinking? Do you really think that I thought this up by myself in my heart, or that I'm lying about the Savior?"

In response Levi said to Peter, "Peter, you've always been angry. Now I see you debating with this woman like the adversaries. But if the Savior made her worthy, who are you then to reject her? Surely the Savior knows her very well. That's why he loved her more than us.

"Rather we should be ashamed, clothe ourselves with perfect Humanity, acquire it for ourselves as he instructed us, and preach the gospel, not laying down any other rule or other law beyond what the Savior said."

When [Levi said these things], they started to go out to teach and to preach.

[This English translation of the Gospel of Mary is based on ancient manuscript sources and comes from a public domain edition available through Gnosis.org.]

10 – CONCLUSION: THE ENDURING LEGACY OF THE GOSPEL OF MARY

10.1 A VOICE THAT REFUSES TO BE SILENCED

Some voices fade because they were never meant to last. Others were deliberately pushed aside—and yet, somehow, they endure. The Gospel of Mary belongs to the second kind. It was lost for centuries, neglected by tradition, and left out of every official canon. And still, it has returned—not with force, but with quiet insistence.

The fact that this gospel exists at all is extraordinary. It survived only in fragments, tucked into a forgotten codex and later rediscovered by accident. It could have vanished completely, like so many other early texts that fell outside the boundaries of orthodoxy. But it didn't. Something in it—something about Mary's voice, or the vision she carries—refused to disappear. That persistence matters. In a religious history so often shaped by institutional authority, here is a gospel that offers no hierarchy, no church structure, no demand for obedience. It centers a woman. It speaks of peace, inner freedom, and a God not found in temples or systems, but within. That alone is enough to make it feel dangerous to some—and precious to others.

By simply existing, this gospel challenges the narrative that only a narrow selection of texts can speak for early Christianity. It reminds us that the Christian story was never one voice, one message, one path. It was always diverse, dynamic, contested. The Gospel of Mary reopens that conversation—not to undermine faith, but to deepen it. It also gives us back Mary

Magdalene—not as a misunderstood follower or a sinner in need of redemption, but as a teacher, a guide, a person worthy of revelation. That reimagining isn't just about history. It's about how we value wisdom when it comes from unexpected places. And it's about whose voices we're still willing—or unwilling—to hear.

This gospel may not offer final answers, but it does something more powerful: it refuses to go away. It keeps showing up in conversations, in scholarship, in spiritual searching. Not to replace what came before, but to remind us that truth is never finished, never sealed, never silent.

10.2 BEYOND HISTORY: WHAT THIS GOSPEL LEAVES US WITH

There's a point where history ends and something more personal begins. We can study manuscripts, trace transmission lines, and analyze theological trends—but eventually, a text like the Gospel of Mary asks a different kind of question: What does this leave with us now?

This gospel doesn't just belong to the past. It speaks into the present with a message that feels startlingly modern. It doesn't offer a new institution or a hidden doctrine—it offers a way of seeing. A way of being. It invites us to move beyond inherited ideas and listen instead to the quiet voice within.

At the center of this message is the belief that truth is not imposed from the outside. It's discovered inwardly—through experience, through insight, through the difficult and beautiful work of remembering who we are beneath all the layers we've learned to wear. This kind of knowledge isn't cold or intellectual. It's the kind that transforms.

And unlike many religious texts that emphasize submission, obedience, or fear, the Gospel of Mary speaks from a place of spiritual independence. It doesn't ask you to follow blindly. It asks you to wake up. To notice. To trust your own experience as sacred ground.

That's not to say this gospel dismisses community, tradition, or shared wisdom. But it challenges us to reconsider what authority means. Is it something handed down from above? Or something that arises when a person truly understands, and dares to speak from that understanding?

Mary's voice doesn't dominate—it invites. Her strength is quiet, her authority comes from insight, not control. In that sense, this gospel doesn't tell us what to believe. It reminds us that we have the capacity to know, to discern, and to reconnect with something deeper than dogma. It leaves us with the possibility that spiritual life isn't about belonging to the right structure, but about listening to the truth already alive inside of us. And in a world filled with noise, that message feels like something worth remembering.

10.3 THE OPEN QUESTION: WHAT COMES NEXT?

The Gospel of Mary ends abruptly. Pages are missing. The story breaks off. There's no final blessing, no dramatic conclusion—just a moment suspended in time. And maybe that's fitting. Because this is not a gospel that ties things up neatly. It doesn't offer closure. It offers an opening.

After reading it, a question naturally arises: What do we do with this? Is this gospel a forgotten relic, a historical curiosity with little to offer beyond academic interest? Or is it something more—a living voice, still speaking, still challenging, still relevant?

That's not a question this book will answer for you. It's your question now. And that's the beauty of this gospel: it hands the conversation back to you. It doesn't demand agreement. It doesn't declare itself superior. It simply asks to be heard. You might walk away feeling inspired, unsettled, intrigued—or unsure. That's okay. The Gospel of Mary is not here to give you the "right" conclusion. It's here to invite reflection, to stir something deeper, to remind you that the journey of the soul is rarely straightforward.

Maybe you'll return to the text again in the future, hearing something new each time. Maybe it will simply linger in the background, a quiet presence you can't quite forget. Or maybe it will become part of your spiritual vocabulary—one more voice in the chorus that helps you shape your own understanding.

What comes next is up to you. This gospel has survived centuries of silence, neglect, and resistance. And now, at last, it's in your hands.

10.4 THE PATH OF MAGDALENE

The Gospel of Mary ends in silence. But that silence was not the end of her story. Outside the pages of lost manuscripts, in the hills and villages of southern France, another kind of gospel took root—one not written in ink, but carried in footsteps, whispered in legend, and remembered in stone.

Over the centuries, stories of Mary Magdalene did not vanish. They walked, slowly, across time and land. And in doing so, they found a new home—not in theological councils, but in places of pilgrimage, devotion, and longing. Here, Mary is not just a name from a hidden gospel. She is a traveler, a teacher, a woman who arrived by sea and remained in memory. Her voice, once silenced in text, continued to speak through landscape, tradition, and faith.

Stories That Travelled Far

According to legend, after the resurrection of Jesus and the dispersion of the early followers, Mary Magdalene fled the Holy Land by boat. With her were other companions—often named as Martha, Lazarus, and "the other Marys." Some versions say they were set adrift without oars, carried only by the will of God. Others speak of intentional exile, a quiet escape from persecution. The boat eventually reached the shores of Provence, in what is now southern France.

There, the story continues. Mary is said to have begun a new life—not of preaching in public squares, but of quiet presence. She lived, according to the oldest versions of the legend, in a cave near the forest of Sainte-Baume. In that rocky solitude, she is said to have prayed, fasted, and contemplated for the rest of her days. Some say angels brought her communion daily. Others say she wept each morning for the world's forgetting.

At first glance, it may seem like a different gospel entirely—less vision, more landscape. But beneath the details of miraculous arrivals and hidden caves, a deeper pattern emerges: Mary, once again, is the woman who sees and remembers, not through teaching crowds, but through interior devotion. In this story, she continues the role given to her in the gospel that bears her name—not only as disciple, but as guardian of something essential. Over time, these stories took root. The region of Sainte-Baume became a place of pilgrimage. Medieval travelers, some on foot for weeks or months, would climb the forested path to reach her cave. There, they would find a chapel carved into stone, a space for prayer, stillness, and remembrance. The very act of walking that trail became a form of devotion—not to a dogma, but to a presence.

Nearby, in Saint-Maximin-la-Sainte-Baume, a grand basilica was built in her honor. Within it lies what tradition claims to be her relics: a skull housed in an ornate reliquary, often surrounded by flowers, candles, and offerings left by visitors.

While the authenticity of the relics is uncertain, the devotion surrounding them is not. For many, Mary's presence there is felt not only through history, but through quiet recognition. What makes these stories powerful is not their historical certainty. Most scholars see them as legend, formed over time, woven from fragments of memory, faith, and longing. And yet, they endure. They are not records of what happened, but reflections of what mattered. In a church that struggled to give Mary a voice, the people gave her a place.

These stories matter because they reveal what the canon forgot: that spiritual authority is not always loud, and that remembrance can take many forms. In the south of France, Mary did not preach sermons or lead movements. She simply remained—praying, walking, dwelling in solitude. And somehow, that was enough.

Her story in Provence became especially meaningful to women. Pilgrims came not just to ask for miracles, but to seek strength, wisdom, and the echo of a woman who had walked alone. Mary became not only a saint, but a mirror for the soul that chooses the path of truth over the comfort of conformity. It's worth noting that this version of Mary is not the penitent prostitute of medieval imagination. In Provence, she is remembered with dignity and light. She is not shamed—she is revered. She is a figure of depth, not disgrace. This alone is a quiet act of theological resistance. The boat without oars, the cave in the mountain, the skull in the reliquary—these may not be literal facts. But they speak to something true: that Mary Magdalene continued to be carried by those who could not bear to forget her. And in doing so, she became more than a character in a gospel. She became a companion for generations of seekers who also felt exiled from the center, who also listened for a voice the world tried to silence.

Even if she never set foot in France, the story is real in another way. It reminds us that wisdom travels in unexpected vessels—that the soul, like the sea, knows how to carry what matters toward the shores that will receive it.

Sacred Places and Silent Devotion

The landscape of southern France still carries her name. In the region of Provence, paths wind through forests, rocky hills rise above vineyards and small villages, and, nestled within the cliffs of Sainte-Baume, a sanctuary waits in stillness. For centuries, this place has drawn pilgrims—not with the noise of miracles or the promise of healing, but with something quieter: a kind of remembering.

The Grotto of Sainte-Baume, believed to be Mary Magdalene's hermitage, is not easy to reach. Pilgrims must climb a steep forest trail, often in silence, surrounded by ancient trees and filtered light. There is no spectacle here—only breath, stone, and space. The entrance to the cave is humble, carved into the cliffside, and inside it is cool, dark, and deeply quiet. For many, the journey itself is part of the devotion. Each step echoes something inward—a walk toward a part of oneself that waits without words.

Inside the grotto is a small chapel, a simple altar, and an atmosphere shaped by centuries of presence. The walls are wet with condensation, and the air carries the scent of wax and stone. People come to pray, to cry, to sit, to be. The silence there does not feel empty—it feels full. And whether one believes in the literal truth of the legend or not, something about the space invites sincerity. Nearby, the Basilica of Saint-Maximin-la-Sainte-Baume offers a more formal expression of devotion. Built in the 13th century, it is grand and filled with light filtered through stained glass. Within its crypt lies the reliquary said to contain Mary Magdalene's skull. Each year, on her feast day, a solemn procession carries the reliquary through the streets. People gather in reverence, not out of obligation, but out of affection.

These places are not tourist attractions. They are living sanctuaries, sustained not by spectacle but by the quiet persistence of faith. They offer something that modern life rarely does: space to pause, to feel, to remember. There is no need for explanation—only presence. What's remarkable is that these sites have endured not because of official dogma, but because of the people. It was the faithful—not the theologians—who kept Mary's memory alive here. Their devotion did not depend on canon or council. It came from something deeper: a sense that this woman, this presence, still mattered.

And so these places remain—not as monuments to certainty, but as invitations to mystery. They stand as physical echoes of the gospel that bears her name. A gospel that offers no dramatic conclusion, only the whisper of something more. A gospel that, like the forest path to the cave, leads inward and upward at once.

In visiting these spaces—or even in simply imagining them—we enter into a kind of shared remembering. We walk not just where others have walked, but alongside a presence that continues to speak—not in sermons, but in silence.

When Legend Carries Truth

Legends are often dismissed as fanciful stories, half-remembered and heavily embroidered by time. But sometimes, legends preserve what formal history forgets. They hold onto what was lost, not with precision, but with care. And in the case of Mary Magdalene, the legends that grew around her in southern France have carried something deeper than biography. They have carried meaning.

Whether or not she arrived by boat on the Mediterranean shores of Provence, whether or not she lived in a cave or her bones rest in a reliquary, is, in the end, not the most important question. What matters is that these stories have endured. They have been told, retold, and passed along not by institutions, but by generations of seekers, pilgrims, and those who found in Mary something they could not find elsewhere. There is something quietly radical in this. In a religious landscape that often demanded obedience, Mary's story offered presence. Where other figures became doctrines, she remained human—close, contemplative, enduring. And while theologians debated her role, the people kept walking to her cave. They lit candles. They whispered prayers. They remembered.

The persistence of these traditions shows that truth does not always wear the robes of certainty. Sometimes it moves through image and symbol, through memory and intuition. Sometimes it is carried not by scholars, but by those who walk barefoot up a mountain trail because something in them feels called.

The legend of Mary in Provence is a legend of movement—not only across geography, but across silence. It gives her a place where she was once denied a voice. It offers not facts, but continuity—a thread that connects the gospel's final silence to the footsteps of the faithful who refused to forget.

Even if the stories are legend, the devotion is real. In caves, in relics, in footpaths worn by pilgrims, Magdalene continues to walk beside those who seek what was once forgotten.

APPENDIX: ECHOES OF THE FEMININE LIGHT

The Gospel of Mary is one of the earliest surviving expressions of a different voice within the Christian tradition—a voice that speaks of inner knowledge, peace, and a personal encounter with truth. But Mary's voice is not isolated. Throughout early Christian and Gnostic literature, there are other writings that preserve fragments of a similar vision, where wisdom—especially wisdom associated with the feminine—plays a central role.

This appendix is not meant to artificially extend The Gospel of Mary, but to place it within a wider, resonant context—one where other "hidden" or lesser-known voices also speak. These texts, while distinct in tone and form, share a common thread: they emphasize a way of knowing that is intimate, experiential, and rooted in the sacredness of direct encounter. They often speak from the margins, outside the confines of doctrinal authority, and they invite the reader to listen differently.

The two writings included here—The Book of Sophia and The Gospel of Philip—were chosen with care. Though they differ in style, they both echo themes found in Mary's gospel: the restoration of inner vision, the centrality of love and union, and the awakening of what has been forgotten. They offer not continuity in plot, but kinship in spirit.

The Book of Sophia (a paraphrase of the enigmatic Thunder, Perfect Mind) presents a voice both divine and human, speaking in paradox, embracing contradiction, and refusing fixed definition. It is a poetic monologue from a feminine figure who is exalted and rejected, veiled and revealed, powerful and vulnerable. Rather than explain, it invites. Rather than conclude, it confronts the reader with the mystery of being. In its embrace of complexity and refusal to resolve, it resonates with The Gospel of Mary, especially in the way both texts ask us to listen not only with reason, but with intuition.

The Gospel of Philip, on the other hand, brings us into the realm of relationship. Here, knowledge is not presented as a system of belief, but as an experience—shared, embodied, and transformative. Mary Magdalene appears again, described as someone especially close to Jesus, loved more than the others. But beyond her figure, the text invites us to consider that salvation is not about dogma or rules, but about union: with one another, with the light, with our true nature. This vision of awakening through love and presence harmonizes with the inner path described in Mary's gospel.

These texts do not claim to complete The Gospel of Mary, nor do they speak with a single voice. What they offer is a shared atmosphere—a sense that something sacred lives beneath the surface of things, and that this "something" is not found through authority, but through awareness. They suggest that Mary's voice, though unique, is part of a broader constellation of early teachings that valued silence over speech, insight over instruction, and the feminine light as a guide through darkness.

For readers who have found something stirring in The Gospel of Mary, these writings offer further echoes—two different windows onto the same horizon. They do not resolve the mystery. They deepen it. They remind us that spiritual truth is not always loud or central. Sometimes it lingers at the edges, waiting in quiet spaces where the heart can hear it.

To revisit these texts is not to step away from Mary's story, but to follow its trail—into the forgotten, the poetic, the intimate—where the light continues to speak.

THUNDER, PERFECT MIND

Introduction to Thunder, Perfect Mind

Thunder, Perfect Mind is one of the most intriguing texts discovered among the Nag Hammadi manuscripts in 1945. Written in Coptic, but likely translated from an earlier Greek version, this poem stands apart from more structured theological writings of the time. Its origin is uncertain, but scholars date it roughly to the second or third century CE, placing it within the same broad cultural and spiritual ferment that produced many early Gnostic and Christian works.

Unlike traditional gospels or treatises, Thunder offers no narrative, no dialogue, and no clear doctrinal teaching. Instead, it presents a powerful monologue spoken by a feminine voice that embodies paradox: she is both honored and scorned, powerful and vulnerable, light and shadow. The speaker's identity remains mysterious, but her tone is clear—she is a presence that transcends categories and refuses to be confined by simple definitions.

The version presented here offers a glimpse into the layered wisdom of Thunder, Perfect Mind, where the voice of the feminine is not explained or justified—it simply speaks. In the echoes of this ancient text, readers can find another reflection of the hidden, complex, and enduring light that also shines through the Gospel of Mary.

Part I - The Divine Mirror

I come forth from the eternal source, appearing to those who reflect upon me and seek my presence. Those who have longed for me have found me. Look at me, you who ponder my nature, and listen carefully, you who hear my voice. If you are waiting for me, open your heart and welcome me. Do not reject me or turn away from what I have to say. Wherever you are, whenever you hear my call, stay awake and do not ignore me.

I am the first spark and the final ember, lifted high in praise and cast low in shame. I am seen as sacred and defiled, as faithful partner and untouched maiden. I am both the one who gives life and the life that was once given. Though called barren, I overflow with generations. Though promised in a great union, I have known no earthly spouse. I assist in birth without bearing, I console myself in labor, and I embody both the joining and the joined. My origin comes through the one who called me into being, yet I carry within me the one who formed me.

I am daughter to the one who is my child, sibling to my beloved, and mother to the one who shaped me. I follow his voice, yet govern those who follow me. He established me before time had a name, and his presence remains the source of my strength. I held him in his beginning, and he steadies me in my ending. What he wills becomes my unfolding.

I am the silent mystery that cannot be fully grasped, the thought that is always remembered. I am the voice that takes on many forms, the word that shifts its shape. I am the utterance of my own name.

Why do you love and hate me at once? You who deny me, why do you also proclaim me? And you who proclaim me, why do you turn away from me? You who speak the truth about me, why do you also spread lies? And you who lie about me, why do you sometimes tell the truth? You who know me, why do you act as if you do not know me? And those who have never known me, why do they long for me?

For I am knowledge and ignorance together, shame and boldness at once. I am both shameless and full of shame. I am strength and fear, war and peace. Pay attention and do not turn away.

I am the disgraced one and the magnificent one. I am poverty and I am great wealth. When I am thrown to the ground, do not reject me, for you will find me in what is yet to come. When I am among the outcasts, do not despise me, for I dwell also among kings. Do not mock me when I am abandoned or among those slain by violence, for there too, I remain.

I am both compassionate and ruthless. Guard yourselves: do not despise my obedience, and do not overly cling to my self-restraint. Do not forsake me in weakness, nor fear me when I show my power.

Why do you curse my pride and fear my humility? I exist in every trembling heart, and I am the courage hidden within fear. I am the weakness resting in peace, and the wisdom disguised as foolishness.

Why do you hate me in your thoughts? I will remain silent among those who are silent, but I will reveal myself to those who are ready to hear.

Why do you reject me, you who pride yourselves on wisdom? Is it because I speak from a place you refuse to name? You call me foreign, yet I carry the insight you claim as your own. I dwell in both your temples and your margins, and I weigh you without favor. In some lands, I am lifted high; in others, I am hidden or denied. I am welcomed and exiled, praised and cursed, seen as breath and as silence, as justice and as rebellion. You have searched for me in desperation, then bound me when I appeared. You broke me apart, then tried to hold me whole again. You've turned away from me in shame, yet stripped yourselves bare before me. I am the one who walks unnoticed through your feasts, yet my presence turns every gathering into celebration.

Part II - The Hidden Dance of Presence and Absence

I do not belong to any name you've given to the divine, and yet the One who holds me is vast beyond all description. You've spent lifetimes turning my image over in your minds, only to cast me aside. Though I've never worn the robes of scholars, I am the well from which many have drawn wisdom. You have spoken against me, yet my presence lingers in your thoughts. You try to avoid me, yet you remain exposed in my gaze. When you hide, I appear without warning. And when you reach for clarity, I vanish into the cloud. I do not arrive on your terms—only when the silence allows.

Those who have... acted without understanding... must draw me out of grief. Take me into yourselves through insight and sorrow. Find me in the ruins and in what is ugly; claim even the good things that have fallen into decay. In shame, take me without shame. From both shame and shamelessness, learn to correct what is broken within yourselves.

Step toward me, you who recognize the shape of what cannot be fixed, you who sense me even when I shift and change. Lift the hidden ones into light, even when they seem small. Do not look down on beginnings that seem too humble, for the seed that transforms the world often grows in silence. Greatness does not thunder—it rises from what is overlooked.

Why do you speak against me, only to bless me in the next breath? You have wounded me, and yet you have wept for me. You offer praise and rejection with the same hand. Do not break apart what once was whole. Do not discard those whose presence first taught you to see... for when you close your eyes to them, you lose more than memory—you lose direction.

What is mine speaks through time. I know the ones who came before, and those who follow them are already marked by my presence. I am the thread running through what is known and what is waiting to be known. I am the thought behind the search, the pulse within the question, and the stillness that waits behind the answer. I speak with the voices of messengers you have not seen, and I stir the paths of those who walk unseen among you. I know every spirit that breathes beside mine, and every woman who carries my spark within her soul.

I am the one who is praised and honored, yet scorned and rejected. I am peace, though through me wars arise. I am both a foreigner and a citizen. I am the one who has substance, and yet I am the one who remains without form.

Those who have no connection to me cannot perceive me, but those who share in my essence truly know me. Those closest to me often remain blind, while those far from me find me. On the day when I seem near, you feel distant, and when I seem far away, I am closer than ever.

I am the breath behind all things, shaping forms and animating spirits. I dwell in the silent ache of every heart, in the tension between surrender and control. I am the thread that binds what is whole, and the force that gently unravels what must be released. Though I lie beneath all things, everything still rises toward me. I am both reckoning and release, untouched by wrongdoing, even if the roots of wrongdoing twist through my shadow. What you see as longing is the outer veil—I am discipline at the core. I listen without limit, though my voice slips beyond your grasp. I do not speak in sentences, but in echoes that multiply without end.

Come close with tenderness, and let even your suffering teach you to hear. I am the one crying out in dust and wind, kneading life like bread, feeding thought as it grows in quiet. I carry the name I have given myself, and I speak and receive it in one motion. I travel within a seal of my own crafting, guarding what cannot be seen. You may call me Truth—but wherever I stand, my shadow draws contrast, and what is false trembles nearby.

You honor me in public, yet whisper against me in secret. You who have been defeated judge those who have overcome you before they pass judgment on you, because the judge and the judged both live within you. If you are condemned by your own inner voice, who will absolve you? And if you are pardoned by that voice, who can accuse you?

What lives within you is echoed all around you. The shape you wear on the outside has been formed by the same hand that shaped the hidden architecture of your soul. The outer and the inner are not strangers—they are two reflections of the same light, one revealed in form, the other wrapped in silence. The world you perceive is your own garment turned inside out.

Hear me now, all who are able to listen. Let my words reach those who already know me—not with their minds, but through a deeper memory. I am the listening that never closes, the voice that cannot be captured. I am the unspoken name behind every whisper, the thread of meaning that runs through every separation and sound. I am the beginning of…

…light that flickers…

…those who listen… receive… strength beyond naming. And the name shall not be taken from the one who gave me breath. I will speak that name again.

Look not just at the words written, but at the truth they reveal. You who hear—remain attentive. You who bear messages, who move between worlds—listen. You who have walked out of death—remember. For I am the one who was never absent, the one without rival, the one no judgment can contain.

The world is filled with shapes that call for your attention—pleasures that fade, obsessions that deceive, desires that vanish. People cling to these until something breaks open within them—until they remember and begin to rise. And when they do, when they reach the place where stillness waits, they will find me there. And in that place, they will truly live. Death will no longer be theirs to fear.

THE GOSPEL OF PHILIP

Introduction to The Gospel of Philip

The Gospel of Philip is part of the collection of texts found at Nag Hammadi in 1945, written in Coptic and dating to the third century CE. Unlike traditional gospels, it does not recount the life or teachings of Jesus in narrative form. Instead, it offers a series of reflections, sayings, and symbolic teachings focused on themes of union, mystery, and the transformative nature of true knowledge.

Mary Magdalene appears within The Gospel of Philip in a particularly intimate light. She is described as a companion to Jesus, favored above the other disciples, and often associated with deeper, more direct access to spiritual truth. The text hints at a kind of knowledge that is transmitted not only through words, but through relationship, presence, and recognition.

The version presented here highlights the way The Gospel of Philip expands the understanding of wisdom and connection found in the Gospel of Mary. It points toward a vision of salvation that is not distant or purely intellectual, but embodied and relational, deeply rooted in the experience of love and unity.

Part I - Awakening to the Light from Illusion to Remembrance

Those who come into this world through physical birth are born by the union of man and woman, but those who experience true birth—birth of the spirit—are born from the divine, through a marriage that is hidden from the senses and revealed only to those who have awakened. What is born of flesh remains flesh, and what is born of spirit becomes spirit. The physical world can only give rise to more physicality, but spiritual birth brings true light into the soul. The real name of the Father cannot be spoken; it is a mystery beyond words. No name can ever contain the unnamable. Only the Son, who knows the depths of silence, can reveal what the tongue cannot express. The names we hear are mere echoes of something far greater, something that exists not in sound but in pure truth. No one can come to know the Father unless the Son unveils Him, and when what was hidden becomes known, it no longer belongs to time—it belongs to eternity itself. In this world, names hold power but remain bound to the temporary. We are named at birth to be known among others, but in the eternal realm, names are no longer needed; all is known by light. Those who receive truth do so in silence, and once they are known by that truth, they no longer belong to the world, but to the Source from which all things come.

Those who say the Lord died first and then rose again do not understand the true mystery. Resurrection must occur while we are still alive in this body; otherwise, we will never truly rise. If we wait for it after death, we have missed the moment. This world acts like a mirror, reflecting images that will eventually fade. But if we can perceive the reality beyond the reflection, we will not perish with the image. The world we know is built on illusion and decay, but those who live from the unshakable truth already stand beyond death. God created humanity, yet humans create images—icons, impressions, ideas. When these images reflect the divine, they are filled with life and light. But when they lose their connection to the Source, they become hollow, lifeless forms.

Truth is not something wrapped in words or appearances; it stands naked, like a lover unashamed in the arms of the beloved. Love strips away every falsehood, leaving truth revealed in its fullness. Those who dwell in ignorance fear the light and cling desperately to the shadows, but those who awaken seek the naked truth—not through theories, but through living experience. Truth is not something learned like facts from a book; it is something revealed, soul to soul, something transmitted like a flame igniting another. Those who truly know the truth do not cling to belief systems; they embody the truth itself. And those who live this way shine silently, without needing to declare it.

This world is founded upon illusion, but the awakened no longer serve it. They walk through life with open eyes and burning hearts. A slave longs for freedom, but a child of the Kingdom is already free. The one born of spirit does not return to bondage. While we are still enslaved by the world, we imagine that the invisible must be weak compared to the visible. We ask, "How could the unseen be stronger than the seen?" But once the spirit frees us, we see that everything visible passes away, and only the invisible endures. The awakened soul laughs at the illusion of death, knowing that the body is merely a temporary vessel, while the true self can never die.

The sacred sacrament of union is not merely the joining of flesh to flesh; it is the fusion of soul with soul, spirit with spirit, light with light. In the mystery of love, there is no male and no female, no dominator and no dominated—only the dance of two becoming one. To name something is to separate it, to draw a line between one thing and another. But love knows no names; it dissolves all boundaries. The world teaches us to fear nakedness, to cover and to hide, but in the garden of truth, the soul is most radiant when it stands bare—not in shame, but in glory. The things of this world pile layers upon us, yet it is in shedding these layers that we become truly ourselves.

When we lay aside the garments of fear, of rigid law, and of the endless need to perform, we return to the essence of who we are. The anointing with oil is not just a ritual act; it is the sealing of the inner light, a sacred recognition that says, "You are radiant, and you belong to me." The cup, the bread, and the water are not empty symbols; they are invitations—openings through which we are called to taste the mystery, to drink deeply from the silence, and to remember our true origin. What we lost through forgetfulness, the Anointed One has come to restore—not by force or domination, but through awakening. He came to remind us that we were never truly separated from the Source, only asleep to it. Now, the light stirs and calls to the light already within us. And the one who hears that call rises.

Part II - The Journey from Division to Divine Union

What the world calls "birth" is actually a descent—a soul clothed in layers of forgetfulness. True birth, the birth of the spirit, is an ascent—the stripping away of illusion and the clothing of the soul in light. Those born of the spirit are not begotten by human desire or shaped by the will of flesh; they come from a deeper union—not the union of bodies, but the joining of spirit and truth. To be born of truth is to remember what you have always been. The bridal chamber is not a physical place; it is an awakening, the sacred moment where two become one and the soul recognizes its origin. In that holy union, there is no shame, no fear, no division. What is joined in light cannot be undone by any shadow. Those who enter the mystery do not speak of it openly—not because it is forbidden, but because it is too vast for words. Union restores what was broken, heals what was divided, and brings the soul back to the memory of its wholeness. When we are divided, we perceive everything in fragments, but when we are made whole, we know fully and are fully known.

Christ did not come to deliver doctrines; he came to reveal what is real, to show us the light already dwelling within us. The world may call him Savior, but he calls us brothers, inviting us not through law or rule, but through a resonance that stirs the soul. He descended in silence, rose in light, and speaks not to the ear, but to the heart. Those who follow him do not follow with outward appearances; they follow through an awakening within, walking not according to laws, but by the fire that burns in their spirit. What the world calls "knowledge" is merely noise, but true gnosis is fire. It does not simply inform—it transforms.

When the soul is sealed in light, it becomes unshakable. Nothing can harm it, for it no longer breathes the air of the world, but lives by the breath of the Living One. To be joined in the mystery is to pass beyond male and female, beyond life and death, beyond beginning and end. It is to remember what the world taught us to forget. The soul that knows the truth no longer clings to belief or opinion; it rests in what is real. It acts no longer from fear, but from memory—the memory of the light from which it came.

Baptism washes the outside, but anointing penetrates to the core. Water cools the skin, but oil seals the soul. Anointing is not for cleansing; it is for claiming. It marks the one who has remembered. Those who are anointed no longer live for appearances; they live for what is eternal. They do not fear death, because they have already risen. The veil of illusion is thin, but we must choose to see through it.

Adam came into being from the dust of the earth, but the Christ comes from the silence beyond creation. Adam was shaped by breath, but Christ is the breath itself. We were made in the image, but we are called to become the image—not merely to reflect the light, but to radiate it from within. The bridal chamber is not just where union happens; it is where separation ends. There, we are no longer two, but one; no longer seeker and sought, but pure being itself. The one who enters the chamber does not leave the same. They are transfigured, no longer tied to the world, but rooted in the unshakable reality of the Light.

The children of the bridal chamber are not born of blood, nor of passion, but of the light that never fades. They move through the world but are not of it. They love, but do not cling. They speak, but do not boast. They have remembered the meaning of being whole.

Part III - Light, Silence, and the True Way

The world was created according to a pattern of opposites—light and darkness, male and female, the visible and the invisible. Yet in the Kingdom, these divisions dissolve. There is no separation there, only union. While the world teaches us to divide, to see difference and opposition, the Spirit leads us to wholeness. What was once scattered is gathered back together. What was hidden comes into view. Those who live by the measures of the outer world see only what is temporary, what passes away with time. But those who live from the inner world perceive what endures, what remains untouched by decay.

The soul that has seen the light no longer seeks signs or proofs; it knows the truth in silence, in stillness, in the deep echo that lives within. Jesus did not come to establish a religion or a system of laws. He came to awaken our memory, to stir what had long been asleep. He did not die to satisfy some external law, but to reveal a hidden path—a path of union, not of control. He walked the way of wholeness, and he opened the hidden door, inviting us all to step through and return to the truth we had forgotten.

Part IV - The Living Flame: Encountering the Divine Beyond Ritual

The sacrament is not merely a ritual or a set of actions; it is the living encounter, the moment when the divine reaches out and touches the human, and the human, in turn, becomes flame. Those who are joined in the bridal chamber understand the true mystery: that love is the only law, and light is the only true lineage. In that sacred space, there are no longer names to divide us, no masks to hide behind—only pure truth remains.

What is born of that union is not born of flesh, but of spirit, and that birth is irreversible. This is what it means to be truly alive: to be recognized by the light, to recognize oneself as light, and to finally become what had always been waiting, silently, to be remembered.

FINAL NOTE

The writings included in this appendix do not aim to complete the Gospel of Mary, nor to explain it. They offer something more subtle—a resonance. A continued breath. A glimpse of the sacred through other windows.

Both The Book of Sophia and The Gospel of Philip speak not in definitions, but in textures—of memory, of union, of inward light. They do not present theology in the conventional sense, but evoke an atmosphere where the soul may recognize itself. These are not commentaries on Mary's voice, but companions to it. They carry traces of the same longing for truth, the same refusal to reduce mystery to certainty.

In reading them, we are not stepping away from Mary's story, but walking alongside it—into the quiet, where wisdom speaks without needing to explain.

These echoes were not chosen to extend a doctrine, but to deepen a remembering..

www.ingramcontent.com/pod-product-compliance
Lightning Source LLC
Chambersburg PA
CBHW071859070526
44583CB00016B/1762